NEW DIRECTIONS FOR CHILD AND ADOLESCENT DEVELOPMENT

William Damon, *Stanford University*
EDITOR-IN-CHIEF

Recent Advances in the Measurement of Acceptance and Rejection in the Peer System

Antonius H. N. Cillessen
University of Connecticut

William M. Bukowski
Concordia University

EDITORS

Number 88, Summer 2000

JOSSEY-BASS
San Francisco

RECENT ADVANCES IN THE MEASUREMENT OF ACCEPTANCE AND REJECTION
IN THE PEER SYSTEM
Antonius H. N. Cillessen, William M. Bukowski (eds.)
New Directions for Child and Adolescent Development, no. 88
William Damon, Editor-in-Chief

Microfilm copies of issues and articles are available in 16mm and 35mm, as well as microfiche in 105mm, through University Microfilms Inc., 300 North Zeeb Road, Ann Arbor, Michigan 48106-1346.

ISSN 1520-3247   ISBN 0-7879-1255-7

NEW DIRECTIONS FOR CHILD AND ADOLESCENT DEVELOPMENT is part of The Jossey-Bass Education Series and is published quarterly by Jossey-Bass Inc., 350 Sansome Street, San Francisco, California 94104-1342. Periodicals postage paid at San Francisco, California, and at additional mailing offices. Postmaster: Send address changes to New Directions for Child and Adolescent Development, Jossey-Bass Inc., 350 Sansome Street, San Francisco, California 94104-1342.

New Directions for Child and Adolescent Development is indexed in Biosciences Information Service, Current Index to Journals in Education (ERIC), Psychological Abstracts, and Sociological Abstracts.

SUBSCRIPTIONS cost $67.00 for individuals and $115.00 for institutions, agencies, and libraries.

EDITORIAL CORRESPONDENCE should be sent to the Editor-in-Chief, William Damon, Stanford Center on Adolescence, Cypress Building C, Stanford University, Stanford, California 94305-4145.

Cover photograph by Wernher Krutein/PHOTOVAULT © 1990.

Jossey-Bass Web address: www.josseybass.com

Printed in the United States of America on acid-free recycled paper containing 100 percent recovered waste paper, of which at least 20 percent is postconsumer waste.

CONTENTS

EDITORS' NOTES

The study of peer relationships in childhood and adolescence continues to play a prominent role in social development research. New problems are investigated, and old problems are considered from new perspectives. With this continued and expanding interest comes a need to revise, reconsider, and redevelop our existing methods to measure peer relations. It is our goal with this volume to contribute to this process by presenting work from various groups of researchers interested in the problems and challenges posed by sociometric methodology. Of course, all of our research on the measurement of peer relations was inspired at one point or another by Jacob Moreno's (1934) original work. Therefore, to place the contributions to this volume in perspective, we begin this volume in Chapter One with a review of Moreno's work and show how developmental psychologists have used the sociometric perspective to understand social development.

The review shows an intense interest in popularity groups in the 1980s, more so than at any time before or since. Although the notion of popularity groups was hardly new, these years were truly the salad days of sociometric classification, with hundreds of sociometric studies reported in journals and at scholarly conferences. The interest in sociometry was primarily practical and functional; it was a way to provide an index of a child's popularity. The lion's share of this research involved sociometric classification.

In this large literature, however, very little attention has been given to the conceptual roots of the concept of popularity. Chapter Two, by Bukowski, Sippola, Hoza, and Newcomb, addresses this issue. These authors propose a conceptual analysis of acceptance, rejection, and social preference and the associations among them. Subsequently, they present empirical evidence that corroborates their conceptual analysis.

An emphasis on the bilateral aspect of sociometry forms the cornerstone of Chapter Three, by Terry, that is presented next in this volume. He discusses a means of measuring popularity that takes into consideration the characteristics of the perceivers who are providing sociometric evaluations. This new development in sociometric measurement clearly builds on Moreno's emphasis on the bilateral nature of liking and disliking. Terry uses this principle to make a distinction between the use of limited versus unlimited nominations to collect sociometric data. The author shows that unlimited nomination methodology is an excellent method for incorporating the role of the perceiver in sociometric research. Terry also clearly shows that certain sociometric choices are not unidimensional, thereby corroborating the conceptual analysis of Bukowski and his colleagues.

Chapter Four, by Maassen, van der Linden, Goossens, and Bokhorst, also addresses the role of the perceiver in sociometric measurement.

Whereas Terry focuses on unlimited nominations as the way to include the perceiver perspective, these authors investigate the use of ratings instead of nominations. They argue that rating scales enable researchers to collect refined information that reflects respondents' actual feelings about their peers in detail. They further demonstrate how their data collection procedure contributes to the identification of sociometric status groups, thus building on and contributing to the development of optimal group identification methods.

In Chapter Five, Cillessen, Bukowski, and Haselager address an issue that is close to Moreno's emphasis on the dynamic nature of groups and sociometric measures. This dynamic nature is reflected in the change and stability of sociometric measures over time. Throughout the history of sociometry, researchers have collected sociometric data longitudinally to assess the reliability and stability of peer status, to examine changes in peer relations across normative changes such as school transitions, and to examine the effects of planned interventions on peer status. For these reasons, consideration of the stability of sociometric status remains an important focus of research. The authors of the final chapter of this volume review what is currently known about the stability of sociometric status categories and address several related conceptual questions.

Collectively, the chapters in this volume address the conceptual and methodological challenges that sociometric measures currently present to the researcher of peer relationships. Although these chapters provide important answers to important questions, they do not include all answers. And they also raise new questions. Although much has been achieved in the sixty-year history of sociometry, further challenges lie ahead. It is our hope that this volume provides the reader with some of the insights and tools that may help us address the future conceptual and methodological challenges of sociometric methods.

Antonius H. N. Cillessen
William M. Bukowski
Editors

ANTONIUS H. N. CILLESSEN is associate professor in the Department of Psychology of the University of Connecticut.

WILLIAM M. BUKOWSKI is professor in the Department of Psychology of Concordia University, Montreal.

1

*The authors describe the evolution of sociometric method-
ology in child development research over the last sixty
years.*

Conceptualizing and Measuring Peer Acceptance and Rejection

Antonius H. N. Cillessen, William M. Bukowski

In this chapter we present an introduction to the basic ideas of Jacob
Moreno's (1934) historical model of sociometric judgment and a brief history of the use of this model in child development research. Our goal is to
show how developmental psychologists have used the sociometric perspective to understand social development. By highlighting the concepts and
ideas that researchers took from Moreno's perspective, as well as what was
left behind, we reveal the strengths and limitations of contemporary sociometric methods. This review provides a conceptual prologue for the subsequent chapters in this volume.

The organization of this chapter is as follows. After introducing the broad
ideas of Moreno's (1934) perspective, we will show how child psychologists initially applied these ideas. We then trace the development of sociometric techniques to study children's peer relations, pointing in particular to the advances
of the past fifteen years. Finally, we discuss the limitations of the techniques that
underlie much of the sociometric "heyday" of the 1980s, and we show the need
for the new perspectives offered in this volume to address these problems.

Basic Ideas Underlying Moreno's Perspective

Four general themes underlie Moreno's (1934) model of sociometric judgment: (1) a focus on two basic dimensions of judgment (attraction and repulsion); (2) a consideration of the perceiver (how one sees others), as well as

The first author was supported by a summer fellowship from the University of Connecticut Research Foundation.

3

the perceived (how one is seen by others); (3) a determination of multiple sociometric constructs; and (4) an emphasis on the dynamic nature of socio-metric data.

First, Moreno believed strongly that interpersonal relationships must be understood via a consideration of two fundamental aspects of interpersonal experience: attractions and repulsions. Moreno defined *attractions* as the positive forces that bring persons together and *repulsions* (or rejections) as the negative forces that keep them apart. Moreno did not see these forces as antithetical or as the opposite ends of a continuum. Instead, he considered them to be two sides of a triangular model for which the third side was the dimension of indifference. According to this model, a person could have feelings of attraction, repulsion, or indifference. In the absence of feelings of attraction to another person, an individual could feel either repulsed or indifferent. Similarly, in the absence of feelings of repulsion, an individual could feel either attracted or indifferent.

Second, Moreno believed that the dimensions of attraction, repulsion, and indifference could be used in two ways to describe an individual's experiences with others. In one way, individuals can be described according to how they are seen by others (the extent to which others are attracted to, repulsed by, or indifferent to them). In another way, individuals can also be described according to how they view members of their peer group (the extent to which the person is attracted to, repulsed by, and indifferent toward others). To assess these views, Moreno simply asked individuals how they felt about associating with each of the members of their peer group. Respondents then indicated whether they liked to associate (attraction), did not like to associate (repulsion), or were indifferent to each of the members of the reference group being considered.

Third, Moreno proposed that how an individual sees others and is seen by others could form the basis of nine dimensions that can be grouped into four sets. Three dimensions referred to the person's feelings toward peers: (1) positive-negative (whether or not the person is attracted to at least one peer); (2) attracted (the person is attracted to three or more peers); and (3) rejects (the person rejects three or more peers). Three others refer to feelings received from peers: (1) isolated (the person is not attractive to at least one peer); (2) attractive (the person is attractive to three or more peers); and (3) rejected (the person is rejected by three or more peers).

Two dimensions refer to the individual's feelings toward immediate group members (for example, classmates) relative to members of related groups (for example, persons in other classes in one's school): (1) extroverted (the person is more attracted to out-group than in-group members) and (2) introverted (more attracted to in-group than out-group members). The last dimension—indifference—refers to the reciprocity between what the person gives and receives (that is, whether the person is indifferent to the majority of the persons who are attracted to or who reject her or him). Moreno used these nine dimensions as the basis of his descriptions of individuals and groups.

The fourth general theme in Moreno's work is his focus on the dynamic nature of groups and the corresponding dynamic nature of sociometric judgments. Because groups are in constant flux, evaluations of persons in groups are changing as well. In addition to his conceptual emphasis of this point, Moreno's earliest empirical work, in which he already examined stability and change in sociometric choices over time, reflects this final theme.

Sociometry and the Study of Child Psychology

The application of Moreno's ideas to the study of children's relations with peers occurred quickly.

The 1940s and 1950s. By the early 1940s, sociometric studies of children's peer groups began to appear in journals (for example, Hunt and Solomon, 1942; Northway, 1940) and researchers set out to refine Moreno's methods (Bronfenbrenner, 1943, 1944). Not all of the ideas in Moreno's model, however, were integrated into research programs. Indeed, three fundamental points disappeared almost completely. First, Moreno's argument that one should consider the person's view of the group (the rejects and attracted dimensions) has never received much attention. Investigators have generally restricted their focus to how the group views the person. Second, researchers have typically spent more time considering the positive dimension (attraction) than the negative one (repulsion). In the earliest sociometric investigations of children's groups (for example, Hunt and Solomon, 1942; Northway, 1940), often only the positive dimension was assessed. Third, in spite of Moreno's insistence on conceptualizing individuals according to nine dimensions, psychologists showed almost immediately a strong desire for a simpler system that would produce a single, final classification for each person.

During the 1940s, sociometric techniques were used as a means of understanding children's social experiences. The concerns that dominated these studies are, for the most part, still with us today. They included (1) the identification of the correlates of sociometric status, typically defined as the extent to which a child was liked by peers, (2) the structure of the peer group, especially patterns of attraction between children of different "groups" (for example, boys and girls), and (3) the refinement of sociometric methods. Of the studies conducted during this period, those that addressed the latter concern have had the most enduring impact. In particular, Bronfenbrenner's (1943, 1944) papers identified a set of issues that are directly pertinent to the advances in sociometric classification that occurred in the late 1970s and early 1980s.

Following earlier remarks by Moreno (1934) and by Jennings (1937), Bronfenbrenner (1943, 1944) saw that in order to make sociometric classification useful for research, a criterion was needed to determine when an individual's acceptance by group members was high (a "star") or low (an "isolate"). Moreno had used the number 3 for this purpose, labeling, for example, persons who were attractive to three or more group members as "attractive." Bronfenbrenner recognized that the use of such a single, absolute criterion was problematic because its meaning would vary across groups as a function of group size, and the number of peers to whom each member of the group was likely to be attracted or repulsed. Indeed, being attractive to three peers has a different order of significance if there are five persons in a group rather than ten and if persons in the group are likely to be attracted to many persons rather than a few. Accordingly, Bronfenbrenner argued that the criterion should be based on statistical considerations and developed a system in which a probabilistic criterion was used to identify persons who were more or less attractive than others.

In Bronfenbrenner's (1943) technique, a person who was attractive to a greater number of peers than expected by chance was assigned to the "stars" group. An individual who was attractive to a lower number of peers (lower than expected by chance) was assigned to the "isolate" group. The development of a procedure for maintaining a constant frame of reference across groups was essential. It allowed researchers to make comparisons across groups, as well as to combine groups to a larger sample adequate for statistical inference. In spite of the value of this technical advance, the procedures recommended by Bronfenbrenner did not permit the consideration of the two fundamental sociometric dimensions of attraction and repulsion simultaneously. Bronfenbrenner notices this problem but his system was not able to solve it.

Lemann and Solomon (1952) observed that the widespread practice of considering only the positive dimension meant that low-accepted children would likely fall into two distinct groups: (1) those who are not accepted and are not rejected and (2) those who are not accepted and are also rejected; a system based only on the positive dimension could not distinguish between rejection and indifference. To solve this problem Lemann and Solomon created a variable to measure indifference. This score was calculated by summing the number of group members who were attracted to the target and the number who rejected the target and then subtracting this sum from the total number of persons in the group (excluding the target individual). With this score and the two fundamental indices, acceptance and rejection, Lemann and Solomon developed a triangular classification taxonomy that assigned children to three groups: (1) high status, that is, children who were high (above a probabilistic criterion) on acceptance and low (below a probabilistic criterion) on rejection; (2) low status, that is, children who were high in rejection and low in acceptance; and (3) average status—all remaining children.

In spite of the apparent advantages of Lemann and Solomon's (1952) taxonomy, it was not used widely. Instead, researchers either continued to rely solely on the positive sociometric dimension or they explored alternative means of measuring acceptance, rejection, and indifference. No one, however, was successful in developing an index that would distinguish between children who were low in attraction and high in rejection and children low in both attraction and rejection.

Both Thompson and Powell (1951) and Dunnington (1957) made some progress in this direction by developing an index of a child's relative likableness. They used a score they referred to as "status" to create three groups (high, medium, and low). The low-status group comprised rejected children only, but the middle group included children who were average in both acceptance and rejection, as well as children who were low on both dimensions. Thompson and Powell and Dunnington themselves recognized this problem with their system. In particular, Dunnington, using a score she labeled "notice" (the sum of received positive and negative choices), found high- and low-status children to be higher in notice than the children in the middle group. Thompson and Powell noted that clearly a solution to this problem was required.

Sociometry's Return: The 1970s and 1980s. Such a solution was not provided for almost thirty years. Peery (1979) described a system of sociometric classification based on the two derivative dimensions (status and notice) described by Dunnington (1957). Peery renamed these dimensions "social preference" and "social impact," respectively, and used them as two orthogonal dimensions that intersected at their means, creating a framework for sociometric classification. With this new model, children could be assigned to four groups: (1) popular (above the mean in impact and preference), (2) rejected (above the mean in impact and below it in preference), (3) amiable (below the mean in impact and above it in preference), and (4) isolated (below the mean in both impact and preference). Although there are several fundamental problems with the specific classificatory scheme that Peery proposed (see Newcomb and Bukowski, 1983), it nevertheless represented a fundamental advance in sociometric classification. Indeed, for the first time researchers had at their disposal a clearly articulated model of sociometric classification that would distinguish between rejected, neglected, and popular children.

A variety of classification systems were developed after Peery's (1979) presentation of his model. According to Crick and Ladd (1989) and Terry and Coie (1991), the most frequently used classification systems are those developed by Coie, Dodge, and Coppotelli (1982) and Newcomb and Bukowski (1983). Although these latter schemes represented important improvements over Peery's technique, they are based on the conceptual framework he developed. The newer techniques have two main advantages. First, they return to the idea of extreme groups discussed by Moreno and Bronfenbrenner. In these new procedures, children who receive very high or very low numbers of nominations are placed in the extreme groups. Coie and others (1982) used a standard score procedure to establish cut-off values, whereas Newcomb and Bukowski (1983) developed cut-offs based on binomial probabilities. Second, these two systems provided for a more differentiated set of groups. These groups are labeled (1) popular—children who receive many positive nominations and few negative nominations (high impact, high preference); (2) rejected—children who receive few positive nominations and many negative nominations (high impact, low preference); (3) neglected—children who receive few positive and negative nominations (low impact); (4) controversial—children who receive many positive and many negative nominations (high impact, mid-range on preference); and (5) average—children who receive an average number of positive and negative nominations (mid-range on both variables).

Limitations with Current Systems

Just as it is important to recognize the advances offered by recent developments in sociometric measurement, it is important to note these flaws also. One way to see the limits of extant methods is to compare them with Moreno's original model. The most significant difference between current techniques and the ideas originally formulated by Moreno is that they provide a single summary index score (a single group classification) for each child, whereas Moreno wished to provide assessment across a set of indicators. Much of this difference derives from the exclusive concern of current researchers with how the peer group views the individual. Moreno was also interested in obtaining information on how the individual viewed the peer group.

Second, like any classificatory procedure that does not rely on naturally occurring cut-off values, sociometric classification is predicated on probabilistic considerations rather than conceptual concerns. Accordingly, the groups that sociometric techniques produce are essentially artificial. They are not arbitrary in the sense that the cut-off scores are capricious or unreasonable, but neither are they natural in the sense that they represent a fundamental property of the peer system. As Dunnington (1957) and Thompson and Powell (1951) pointed out, the cut-offs used to designate groups are designed to make statistical sense rather than to correspond to an underlying psychological meaning. That is, the criteria reflect levels of statistical infrequency rather than functional or conceptual demarcations. More important, the variables on which sociometric classifications are based (the underlying dimensions of preference and impact) are continuous variables. The sensitivity of a continuous measure is lost when it is parsed to serve the needs of a procrustean classification procedure.

Third, the groups that are obtained with a sociometric technique differ along multiple dimensions. In some comparisons, however, two groups differ along more than one dimension. The popular and rejected groups, for example, differ on both acceptance and rejection. Accordingly, adjustment differences between these two groups may be due to variations in either acceptance or rejection. Moreover, one would not know if, for example, rejected children's difficulties derive from the fact that many people dislike them or from the fact that the number of people who dislike them is disproportionate to the number of people who like them. To some extent, more focused contrasts among groups can address some of these issues. Rejected children and controversial children, for example, are both high-impact groups who have many people who dislike them. However, controversial children also have many people who like them, whereas rejected children do not. Thus, comparing these groups can isolate the effect of being accepted, at least in the context of being highly disliked.

Finally, Moreno's sociometry was bilateral. He emphasized the importance of knowing whether children liked the particular children who liked them, and whether the peers a child liked also liked the child in return. Today's sociometry is, by contrast, largely unilateral; emphasizing how a child is seen by the group and placing no emphasis on how the child sees the group. This is a significant shortcoming.

Our review of the principles and development of sociometry shows that much has been achieved in the measurement of the peer system. Yet, in spite of the achievements, sociometric measurement continues to provide challenges and inspire new developments. The analyses of the conceptual roots of popularity, the role of perceiver characteristics, the use of rating and nomination techniques, and the stability of sociometric status in the four chapters that lie ahead represent four of these new developments. They clearly build on the history of sociometric measurement but also show how this important technique can be improved for new research on child and adolescent peer relations.

References

Bronfenbrenner, U. "A Constant Frame of Reference for Sociometric Research." *Sociometry*, 1943, *6*, 363–397.

Bronfenbrenner, U. "A Constant Frame of Reference for Sociometric Research: II. Experiment and Inference." *Sociometry*, 1944, *7*, 40–75.

Coie, J. D., Dodge, K. A., and Coppotelli, H. "Dimensions and Types of Social Status: A Cross-Age Perspective." *Developmental Psychology*, 1982, *18*, 557–570.

Crick, N. R., and Ladd, G. W. "Nominator Attrition: Does It Affect the Accuracy of Children's Sociometric Classifications?" *Merrill-Palmer Quarterly*, 1989, *35*, 197–207.

Dunnington, M. J. "Investigation of Areas of Disagreement in Sociometric Measurement of Preschool Children." *Child Development*, 1957, *28*, 93–102.

Hunt, J. M., and Solomon, R. L. "The Stability and Some Correlates of Group Status in a Summer Camp Group of Young Boys." *American Journal of Psychology*, 1942, *55*, 33–55.

Jennings, H. H. "Structure of Leadership-Development and Sphere of Influence." *Sociometry*, 1937, *1*, 99–143.

Lemann, T. B., and Solomon, R. L. "Group Characteristics as Revealed in Sociometric Patterns and Personality Ratings." *Sociometry*, 1952, *15*, 7–90.

Moreno, J. L. *Who Shall Survive? A New Approach to the Problem of Human Interrelations.* Washington, D.C.: Nervous and Mental Disease Publishing Co., 1934.

Newcomb, A. F., and Bukowski, W. M. "Social Impact and Social Preference as Determinants of Children's Peer Group Status." *Developmental Psychology*, 1983, *19*, 856–867.

Northway, M. L. "Appraisal of the Social Development of Children at a Summer Camp." *University of Toronto Studies, Psychology Series*, 1940, *5*(1), 62.

Peery, J. "Popular, Amiable, Isolated, Rejected: A Reconceptualization of Sociometric Status in Preschool Children." *Child Development,* 1979, *50,* 1231–1234.

Terry, R., and Coie, J. D. "A Comparison of Methods for Defining Sociometric Status Among Children." *Developmental Psychology,* 1991, *27,* 867–880.

Thompson, G., and Powell, M. "An Investigation of the Rating-Scale Approach to the Measurement of Social Status." *Educational and Psychological Measurement,* 1951, *11,* 440–455.

ANTONIUS H. N. CILLESSEN is associate professor in the Department of Psychology of the University of Connecticut.

WILLIAM M. BUKOWSKI is professor in the Department of Psychology of Concordia University, Montreal.

2

The association between acceptance and rejection measured with nominations is not adequately described by a simple linear relationship. Sociometric ratings measure social preference but can also yield indicators of acceptance and rejection.

Pages from a Sociometric Notebook: An Analysis of Nomination and Rating Scale Measures of Acceptance, Rejection, and Social Preference

William M. Bukowski, Lorrie Sippola, Betsy Hoza, Andrew F. Newcomb

Sociometry has had a prominent place in the research literature on children's social development. It has been used widely in the study of peer relations as both a technique for measuring the positive and negative forces among children and as a conceptual scheme for understanding the basic processes of the peer system. Beginning with Moreno's landmark publications (for example, Moreno, 1934), sociometry has been used by social developmentalists interested in peer relations as a powerful empirical and conceptual tool. In spite of sociometry's rich conceptual and methodological heritage, however, some issues regarding the use of sociometric measures remain unresolved and, in some cases, unexamined.

In this chapter we address two of these unresolved issues: (1) how the two sociometric constructs—acceptance and rejection—are related to each other and to other sociometric constructs and (2) whether nomination and rating scale measures index the same constructs. The main focus of the second issue concerns which sociometric construct is measured by the mean received liking-disliking rating measure. These issues are fundamental to the study of children's experience within the peer group in that they involve the nature of sociometric constructs and the techniques by which these constructs are measured.

NEW DIRECTIONS FOR CHILD AND ADOLESCENT DEVELOPMENT, no. 88, Summer 2000   © Jossey-Bass

For each of these issues, however, concerns, unresolved questions, and even outright confusions can be seen in the literature; our goal in this chapter is to resolve some of these. We do this in two ways, first by means of a conceptual analysis of the constructs and then via an empirical analysis of hypotheses derived from the conceptual analysis.

Issue 1: Interrelationships Between Two Sociometric Constructs—Acceptance and Rejection

The first issue we consider is the nature of the association between acceptance and rejection. We examine how these constructs are related to each other and how each is related to the derivative sociometric construct of social preference. As part of our consideration of this issue, we examine different techniques that have been used to measure acceptance and rejection.

Although there may be uncertainty about some aspects of sociometric theory and technique, there is no disagreement that a sociometric analysis should account for the two fundamental sociometric dimensions of acceptance and rejection (Newcomb and Bukowski, 1983). *Acceptance* refers to the number of strong positive links a child has with other members of the peer group; *rejection* refers to the number of negative links a child has with other members of the group. The links indexed by acceptance are experienced by children as a positive form of affect associated with their desire to be with someone else. In this respect, acceptance is largely, if not completely, synonymous with liking and is a basic property of friendship.[1] The rejection links are a negative form of affect associated with a child's desire to stay away from another child. Rejection is largely, if not completely, synonymous with disliking. Each of these constructs is a dimensional entity rather than a category, in the sense that children can vary from one another in the degree to which they are accepted or rejected by peers. They don't simply fall into either an accepted or rejected group.

Relationship Between Acceptance and Rejection. Acceptance and rejection are related to each other but not as polar opposites. That is, the opposite of acceptance is not rejection, and the opposite of rejection is not acceptance. Instead, the opposite of being liked is not being liked, and the opposite of being disliked is not being disliked. As discussed earlier in this volume, Moreno (1934) showed that one could conceive of a triangular model consisting of three conceptual anchors: acceptance, rejection, and indifference. Indifference refers to a condition in which a child is neither liked nor disliked.

Consider that in a group there are likely to be three extreme kinds of persons (see Newcomb and Bukowski, 1983): (1) those who are highly liked by many of their peers and disliked by few, (2) those who are disliked by many and liked by few, and (3) those who are liked by few and disliked by few. The conditions represented by the first two groups imply that liking and disliking (or acceptance and rejection) are indeed antagonistic concepts. The third group, however, shows that this is not necessarily so. That is, not being liked (the absence of liking) is not synonymous with being disliked, and not being disliked (the absence of disliking) is not synonymous with being liked. In this way, the absence of attraction does not imply the presence of repulsion, and the absence of repulsion does not imply the presence of attraction.

Accordingly, among the persons who are low in acceptance one would expect to find persons who are high in rejection as well as those who are low in rejection; likewise, among the persons who are low in rejection one should find persons who are high in acceptance as well as persons who are low in acceptance. In light of this, persons who are low in acceptance are heterogeneous on the dimension of rejection (that is, some are high in rejection, others are not), and persons who are low in rejection are heterogeneous on the dimension of acceptance (that is, some are high in acceptance, others are not).

If it were simply the case that persons who were low in rejection were also high in acceptance and that persons low in acceptance were also high in rejection, then the association between rejection and acceptance would be linear and negative. This linear relationship is challenged, however, by the heterogeneity on the dimension of acceptance at the low end of rejection and the heterogeneity in rejection at the low end of acceptance. This heterogeneity at the low end of acceptance and at the low end of rejection means that a simple linear relationship does not explain how these variables are related to each other. Instead, it is likely that a curve in this association would account for the heterogeneity at the low ends of each of these dimensions.

Put simply, this conceptual analysis implies that there should be (1) a negative linear relationship between acceptance and rejection, as well as (2) a curvilinear relationship between them. That is, one would expect the association to have a largely negative slope but with steeper trajectories at the upper and lower levels. The curvilinear association would represent the heterogeneity in rejection at the low end of acceptance, as well as the heterogeneity in acceptance at the low end of rejection. Accordingly, the trajectory of the association between acceptance and rejection would be steepest at high levels of rejection.

An examination of the linear and curvilinear associations between acceptance and rejection constitutes the first question we address in the current report. We examine this issue by (1) assessing the strength of the linear and curvilinear links between acceptance and rejection and (2) comparing the variances of the acceptance and rejection scores of children who fall at the low ends of these dimensions.

Derivative Sociometric Constructs. In addition to their utility for representing the two basic social forces of acceptance and rejection, these fundamental measures can be combined to form two derivative constructs— social preference and impact (Coie, Dodge, and Coppotelli, 1982; Newcomb and Bukowski, 1983). (As social preference appears to be a more powerful dimension than impact, we will focus on it in this chapter.) Preference is a measure of relative likableness. The relative part of this construct concerns the difference between the number of positive and negative links a person has with others or the difference between how much they are liked and disliked. Persons who are high in social preference are liked (accepted by or attractive to others) more than they are disliked (rejected by or repulsive to others); persons who are low in social preference are disliked (or rejected-repulsive) more than they are liked (or accepted-attractive).

In contrast to what is seen with the dimensions of acceptance and rejection, little heterogeneity is to be expected at the end points of the preference measure. Persons at each end are likely to be homogeneous on both acceptance and rejection. That is, all persons with high preference scores are likely to have high acceptance scores and low rejection scores, whereas these who are low in preference are all likely to have low acceptance scores and high rejection scores. At the center of the distribution of the preference dimension, however, high levels of heterogeneity across the acceptance and rejected scores are expected. Some persons will be high on both scores; some will be low on both; others will be at the midpoint on both. In this respect, the derivative nature of the construct of preference makes it an odd conceptual and psychometric entity. Like other difference scores, it is a single construct that reflects two underlying constructs that are neither synonymous with nor independent of each other.

An empirical assessment of this conceptual analysis of how acceptance and rejection are related to preference and impact constitutes the second question we address in this report. We examine the degree of variance on measures of acceptance and rejection among children who are at the extreme ends of the dimension of preference.

Issue 2: Do Nomination and Rating Scale Measures Index the Same Constructs?

Typically, two measurement techniques have been used to measure sociometric constructs. One relies on a nomination procedure whereas the other employs a rating scale.[2] Questions regarding the utility of different measurement procedures for indexing sociometric constructs such as preference or impact have been seen in the literature for over fifty years. Currently, it is not clear whether these two procedures provide information about the same underlying constructs or if each technique is uniquely suited to index one construct rather than another. In this section we describe these two techniques and discuss how they have been used. We then provide a conceptual analysis to support our assertion that each technique can be used to produce indices of acceptance, rejection, and preference.

Nomination Techniques. Nomination techniques index acceptance and rejection through independent questions. Typically, participants in a nomination sociometric assessment are asked to identify (1) the persons to whom they are most attracted (those they like most or whom they think of as their friends) and (2) the persons by whom they are repulsed or whom they reject (those they dislike or with whom they do not wish to associate). The number of times a person is identified in response to the first question is used as an index of acceptance, and the number of times a person is identified in response to the second question is used as an index of rejection. These scores are typically standardized to control for variations in the number of persons in the nominating pool and to ensure that each score has the same variance.[3] The nominating pool is typically used as the reference group for computing the appropriate mean and standard deviation for the standardization procedure. These standardized acceptance and rejection scores are used to create measures of sociometric preference and impact. The sociometric preference score is computed by (1) subtracting the standardized rejection score from the standardized acceptance score and then (2) standardizing the difference. Impact is computed by adding the standardized acceptance and rejection scores and standardizing the sum.

Rating Scales. When the rating scale technique is used, participants are asked to evaluate each of their peers on a rating scale anchored by terms representing liking and disliking. Usually, a scale consisting of 3, 5, or 7 points is used. One end of the scale is labeled "like very much," and the other end is labeled "dislike very much." At least two and perhaps three types of scores can be computed with these scores. The best known of these scores is a mean score computed for each child based on the ratings the child receives from peers. A second score, originally described by Asher and Dodge (1986), is a sum indicating the number of times a child received the lowest possible rating on the scale. A third score would be the converse of this, specifically a sum indicating the number of times a child received the highest possible rating. Our present interest in these scores concerns the specific sociometric construct they index.[4]

The first of these scores, that is the mean of the ratings each child receives, has already been referred to by the name *acceptance,* implying that it measures the same construct as the nomination-based measure by the same name. Nevertheless, from a conceptual perspective it appears that this measure more closely resembles the construct of social preference than that of acceptance.

This position is based on the following two points. First, the mean received liking rating is derived from a rating scale measure that invokes the concepts of both liking and disliking. Indeed, terms that refer to liking and disliking typically serve as the anchor points on these scales. Accordingly, the mean received score taken from such scales includes a "mixture" of the entire range of scores (high, low, and mid-range) that a child receives. This reliance on the balance between liking and disliking is, of course, a central feature of the construct of social preference.

Second, as with the nomination measure of social preference, one would expect that children with high mean received liking-disliking ratings would be those who receive many high ratings and few low ratings, making them homogeneous on both acceptance and rejection. Similarly, one would expect that children with low mean received liking-disliking ratings would be those who receive few high scores and many low scores, making them homogeneous on acceptance and rejection. In the middle range there would be a heterogeneous group of persons who vary considerably in terms of the number of positive and negative links they have with others and in terms of the amount of liking and disliking they experience. These characteristics exactly parallel the characteristics of the nomination-based social preference measure.

Considering these two points, we propose 'that the mean received rating score appears to bear a stronger resemblance to the construct of preference than to any of the other three sociometric dimensions (acceptance, rejection, or impact). If this is the case, then one would expect that the mean received rating score will show greater empirical similarity to the nomination-based measure of social preference than to the nomination-based measures of acceptance and rejection. The empirical analysis constitutes the central focus of the second set of analyses reported in this chapter. That is, we examine whether the mean received rating score is more strongly correlated to the nomination-based social preference measure than it is to the nomination-based measure of acceptance and the nomination-based measure of rejection.

Asher and Dodge (1986) identify the second measure (the sum indicating how often a child received the lowest, or most negative, rating on the scale) as an index of rejection. They support this view by showing that this index has the same conceptual and functional properties as the nomination-based rejection measure. On the conceptual side, they show that both measures are indices of disliking. On the functional-empirical side, they show that the nomination-based and rating-scale-based measures are highly correlated and are related to other variables in parallel ways. Accordingly, it appears that these two measures are indices of the same construct.

This same conceptual analysis can be used to interpret the third score we described—the sum indicating how often the child received the highest or most positive rating. Just as the lowest scores on a liking-disliking rating scale are measures of rejection (evidence of negative links between a person and peers), it is reasonable to expect that the highest ratings may be indices of acceptance (evidence of positive links between a person and peers). If the number of highest ratings that a person receives from peers on a rating scale is a measure of acceptance, then one would expect that (1) it would be highly correlated with the standard measure of acceptance (the number of received positive sociometric nominations), and (2) its associations with other measures would parallel those of the standard measure of acceptance.

In summary, we make three proposals regarding the constructs indexed by the rating-scale-based measures: (1) that the mean received rating scale measure is an index of sociometric preference, (2) that the score indexing the number of times a child receives the lowest possible rating score is a measure of rejection, and (3) that the score indexing the number of times the child receives the highest possible rating is a measure of acceptance. An examination of these conceptually based proposals represents the second portion of the empirical part of this report. In these analyses we examine whether each rating scale measure is more highly correlated to the nomination measure to which we propose it corresponds than to the other nomination measures.

Summary. An examination of the associations between acceptance and rejection constitutes the first question we address in this report. We examine the issue by assessing the strength of the linear and curvilinear links between acceptance and rejection and by comparing the variances of the acceptance and rejection scores of children who fall at the low ends of these dimensions. Variance in both acceptance and rejection was examined also for the participating children who were high in preference and for those who were low in preference.

The second issue considered here concerns the associations between nomination-based and rating-scale-based sociometric measures. Specifically, we examined the hypotheses that (1) the mean of the liking-disliking ratings that a child receives from peers is an index of social preference; (2) the score indexing the number of times a child receives the lowest possible rating is a measure of rejection; and (3) the score indexing the number of times the child receives the highest possible rating is a measure of acceptance. These issues are examined in two samples of early adolescent boys and girls.

Samples. In each of two samples, the sociometric constructs of acceptance, rejection, and preference were measured with both nomination and rating scale techniques. Sample 1 consists of five hundred third-grade ($n = 147$), fourth-grade ($n = 105$), and fifth-grade ($n = 228$) boys ($n = 239$) and girls ($n = 261$) from twenty classrooms in five schools. Participants completed a nomination-based sociometric questionnaire in which they identified the three same-sex participating classroom peers whom they liked the most and the three they disliked the most. They also completed a rating scale sociometric questionnaire. The anchors of the 5-point scale used in the rating assessment were "dislike" and "like very much."

With the nomination data, we computed three scores: (1) a traditional measure of acceptance (number of times the child was nominated for the "like most" sociometric question), which was standardized within sex and class; (2) a traditional measure of rejection (number of times the child was nominated for the "dislike most" sociometric question), which was standardized within sex and class; and (3) a measure of sociometric preference, computed by subtracting the standardized nomination-based measure of rejection from the standardized nomination-based measure of acceptance. This final score was then standardized within sex and class.

Three scores were also computed with the rating scale data: (1) the mean of the liking-disliking ratings received from peers, (2) a sum indicating how often the child was given a rating of 5 (the highest possible rating), and (3) a sum indicating the number of times the child was given a rating of 1 (the lowest possible rating). The first of these scores is expected to be a measure of sociometric preference, the second a measure of sociometric acceptance, and the third a measure of sociometric rejection (see Asher and Dodge, 1986). As with the nomination-based scores, these scores were standardized within sex and class.

Although the same procedures used with Sample 1 were generally used with Sample 2, there were some important differences. The boys and girls in Sample 2 were part of a longitudinal study. At Time 1 (T1), there were 131 girls and 105 boys in grades three, four, and five. This assessment was held in May of the school year. Time 2 (T2) occurred nineteen months later, during early December of the following school year when the participants were in grades five, six, and seven. At this time there were 130 girls and 105 boys in the sample, 88 percent of whom had also participated at T1. Time 3 took place in May of this same school year, five months after T2 and twenty-four months after T1. In this sample there were 126 girls and 105 boys at this time. Of these children, 87 percent were also participants at T1, and 97 percent had participated at T2. At each of these three times, an unlimited number of same-sex choices was permitted in both the positive and negative nomination sociometric procedures. As in Sample 1, a liking-disliking rating scale was used in addition to the nomination procedures. The size of the nominating pool in Sample 2 was smaller than in Sample 1. At T1 there were, on average, 8.7 same-sex peers in the nominating pool, whereas at T2 and T3 the corresponding figures were 6.9 and 7.4. Three nomination-based scores and three rating scale scores were computed as in Sample 1.

Analysis of Issue 1

Our first two sets of analyses were conducted to empirically examine the association between acceptance and rejection. We first used multiple regression to assess the presence of the hypothesized linear (negative) and curvilinear associations between acceptance and rejection. We examined also the degree of variability in acceptance and rejection scores among the children who had extremely low scores on acceptance or rejection to assess whether the predicted patterns of homogeneity would be observed. These analyses were conducted with both the nomination and rating scale measures.

Linear and Curvilinear Association Between Acceptance and Rejection. The linear and curvilinear links between acceptance and rejection were examined with the partialed powers technique described by Cohen (Cohen, 1978; Cohen and Cohen, 1983). In these analyses, we used rejection as the dependent measure; acceptance and its square (acceptance multiplied by acceptance) were used as predictors entered, in this order, on two successive steps. The presence of a linear association would be shown by the significance of the first term, and the presence of a curvilinear effect would be shown by the significance of the second term. Two analyses were conducted with the Sample 1 data, one using the nomination-based measures and one using the rating scale data. These same analyses were conducted also with the Sample 2 data, with separate analyses being conducted with the nomination and rating data at each of the three times, resulting in a total of six analyses.

Each of the analyses revealed the predicted linear and curvilinear effects. To illustrate this effect, we report the findings from four analyses, two from Sample 1 and two analyses conducted with the measures from T1 with Sample 2. (These findings are consistent with those obtained at the other times with Sample 2.) With the Sample 1 nomination-based scores, the effect of the acceptance measure was, as predicted, significant and negative, $F(1, 498) = 138.82$, $p < .001$, $R = .46$, $\beta = -.46$. The effect of the squared acceptance score (the curvilinear effect) was also significant after the linear association had been controlled for, $F_{change}(1, 497) = 16.52$, $p < .001$, $\beta = .17$. The final β of the acceptance score was $-.54$, and the final R for the model was .50. The same pattern was observed with rating scale measures. The linear effect of the rating scale acceptance measure (that is, the number of highest ratings received) was significant and negative, $F(1, 498) = 184.57$, $p < .001$, $R = .52$, $\beta = -.52$, and the effect of the squared acceptance score was also significant, $F_{change}(1, 497) = 53.62$, $p < .001$, $\beta = .28$. The final β of the acceptance score was $\beta -.61$, and the final R for the model was .59. The pattern of association represented by these findings is shown in Figure 2.1.

The findings for the measures from T1 with Sample 2 showed these same patterns. With the nomination data, the linear effect of the acceptance

Figure 2.1. Association Between Acceptance and Rejection in Sample 1 (T1) and Sample 2 Using Nominations and Ratings

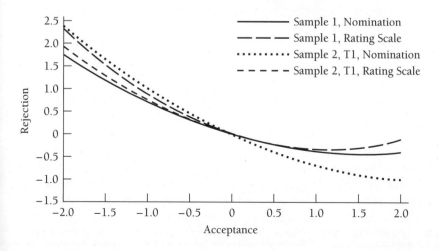

variable was negative and significant, $F(1, 230) = 806.82, p < .001, \beta = -.88$, $R = .79$, and the effect of the squared acceptance score was also significant, $F_{change}(1, 229) = 3.65, p < .05, \beta = .07$. The final β of the acceptance score was $-.85$, and the final R for the model was .78. With the rating scale measures, the linear effect of the acceptance variable was negative and significant, $F(1, 216) = 96.94, p < .001, R = .56, \beta = -.56$, and the effect of the squared acceptance score was also significant, $F_{change}(1, 229) = 12.25, p < .001, \beta = .20$. The final β of the acceptance score was $-.57$, and the final R for the model was .59. These findings are represented in Figure 2.1. Findings identical to these were seen with the Sample 2 data at T2 and T3. Overall, these findings provide empirical confirmation for the conceptual analysis presented earlier, indicating both a negative linear association and a curvilinear association between acceptance and rejection.

Differential Variability in Acceptance and Rejection. A second set of analyses focused on the heterogeneity in acceptance at the low end of rejection and the corresponding heterogeneity in rejection at the low end of acceptance. In an attempt to empirically confirm this hypothesized heterogeneity, we calculated the variance in acceptance and rejection for the children who were at the low ends (had a score of less than or equal to -1) on these dimensions. Variances were calculated for both the nomination and rating measures at each time in both samples. We also calculated these values at both the high (> 1.0) and low (< -1.0) ends of the preference dimension. We report only the findings from Sample 1 and from T1 of Sample 2. The remaining findings are parallel to those we report.

As shown in Table 2.1, the findings indicate the following. First, at the low end of the acceptance dimension, the observed variance in the rejection scores was substantially higher than the observed variance in the acceptance scores. (As these scores were standardized, the expected variance estimate would be 1.0.) That is, for the children who were low in acceptance, the variance in rejection was, on average, thirty-one times larger than the variance in acceptance. Second, at the low end of rejection, the variance in acceptance was, in all cases, larger than the variance in rejection. That is, for the children who were low in rejection, the variance in acceptance was, on average, twenty-one times larger than the variance in rejection. If acceptance and rejection were opposites of each other, one would have expected that (1) at the low end of acceptance the variance observed in acceptance would have been equal to the variance observed in rejection and (2) at the low end of rejection the variance in rejection would be equal to the variance in acceptance, and (3) these variance measures would be very small. Our findings show clearly that none of these three conditions was met.

The amount of variance on the measures of acceptance and rejection at high and low levels of preference was studied next. Our comparisons showed clearly that at both the high and low levels of sociometric preference, the amount of variance in acceptance and the amount of variance in rejection were

Table 2.1. Variance of Acceptance and Rejection at High and Low Preference and Low Acceptance and Rejection

Participants	Type of Measure	Acceptance	Rejection
Sample 1	Nomination	.12	.20
Low Preference	Rating	.11	.24
Sample 1	Nomination	.25	.19
High Preference	Rating	.26	.14
Sample 1	Nomination	.03	1.76
Low Acceptance	Rating	.06	1.74
Sample 1	Nomination	.80	.03
Low Rejection	Rating	.75	.07
Sample 2, T1	Nomination	.13	.14
Low Preference	Rating	.18	.31
Sample 2, T1	Nomination	.05	.06
High Preference	Rating	.23	.08
Sample 2, T1	Nomination	.11	.52
Low Acceptance	Rating	.05	1.67
Sample 2, T1	Nomination	.62	.18
Low Rejection	Rating	1.49	.03

not only small but were roughly equivalent. For example, in Sample 1, among the children who were low in preference, the variance in the measure of acceptance was .12 and the variance in the measure of rejection was .20. (Keep in mind that the overall variance in these measures was 1.0.) The variance on these measures was greater than .25 in only three of the sixteen observations performed (four observations with Sample 1 and four observations at each of T1, T2, and T3). Clearly, among the children at the high and low levels of preference, there is (1) relatively little variance in acceptance and rejection and (2) roughly equal variance in the acceptance and rejection scores of these children.

Analysis of Issue 2

We conducted the next set of analyses to assess whether the mean received rating scale score was more strongly related to the nomination-based sociometric measure of preference, as we hypothesized, than to the nomination-based measure of acceptance, as others have implied (Parker and Asher, 1993). The correlations between the mean received rating and these two measures are presented in Table 2.2. Using the procedure developed by Meng, Rosenthal, and Rubin (1992), we compared the size of the correlation between the mean received rating score and the standard nomination-based measure of preference with the correlation between the mean received rating score and the nomination-based measure of acceptance.

As shown in Table 2.2, the z-score statistic produced by the Meng and others' formula reveals that with the Sample 1 data and at each of T1, T2, and T3 with Sample 2, the mean received liking-disliking rating score was

Table 2.2. Correlations Between the Mean Received Liking Ratings and the Nomination Measures of Acceptance and Preference

Sample	r with acceptance	r with preference	z for differences between r's
Sample 1	.58	.77	11.11
Sample 2, T1	.77	.89	9.81
Sample 2, T2	.79	.89	10.11
Sample 2, T3	.81	.90	8.61

significantly more strongly associated with the nomination-based measure of social preference than with the nomination-based measure of acceptance (all p's < .001). The correlations between the mean received liking-disliking rating and the acceptance measure was strong, indicating an overlap between them of about 33 percent in Sample 1 and 60 percent in Sample 2. (The difference between the samples was probably due to the use of a limited sociometric procedure in Sample 1 and an unlimited procedure in Sample 2.) This degree of association is to be expected, considering that preference is in part derived from acceptance. The overlap between the mean received rating score and the nomination-based preference measure was 60 percent in Sample 1 and over 75 percent in Sample 2. This pattern of findings shows that the overlap between the mean received ratings score and the nomination-based preference measure is larger than the overlap between it and the nomination-based acceptance measure by nearly 90 percent in Sample 1 and by about 25 percent in Sample 2.

These findings show clearly that the mean received liking-disliking rating is more strongly related to the standard measure of social preference than it is to the standard measure of acceptance. These findings, in conjunction with the conceptual analysis discussed earlier, provide strong support for the proposal that the mean received rating score measures the construct known as sociometric preference rather than the construct known as acceptance.

We also used Meng and others' (1992) technique to assess the hypotheses that (1) the number of times a child receives the lowest possible rating score is a measure of rejection, and (2) the number of times a child receives the highest possible rating is a measure of acceptance. For each of these two measures we examined whether it was more strongly related to the nomination measure to which we presumed it would correspond than to the nomination-based measure of social preference. Four comparisons were made with each variable, one with Sample 1 and then one at each of T1, T2, and T3 with Sample 2.

As shown in Table 2.3, with each of the four comparisons the rating scale measure of rejection was more strongly related to the nomination-based measure of rejection than to the nomination-based measure of social preference. A parallel set of findings was observed with the rating scale measure presumed to index acceptance (see Table 2.4). It was more strongly associated to the

Table 2.3. Correlations Between the Rating Measure of Rejection and the Nomination Measures of Rejection and Preference

Sample	r with rejection	r with preference	z for differences between r's[1]
Sample 1	.70	−.61	5.06
Sample 2, T1	.60	−.52	2.74
Sample 2, T2	.76	−.64	4.60
Sample 2, T3	.73	−.67	4.58

Note: [1]The difference was tested between the correlation with rejection and the absolute value of the correlation with preference.

Table 2.4. Correlations Between the Rating Measure of Acceptance and the Nomination Measures of Acceptance and Rejection

Sample	r with acceptance	r with preference	z for differences between r's
Sample 1	.65	.57	2.99
Sample 2, T1	.79	.72	2.60
Sample 2, T2	.76	.64	4.04
Sample 2, T3	.68	.58	2.80

nomination-based measure of acceptance than to the nomination-based measure of social preference. Each of these sets of comparisons supports the argument that rating scale and nomination techniques can be used to produce conceptually valid and empirically validated indices of acceptance, rejection, and social preference.

Summary and Discussion

In this chapter we address questions regarding the association between acceptance and rejection and between nomination-based and rating-scale-based measures of acceptance, rejection, and preference. Our goal in examining these issues was to address some fundamental problems regarding the associations between sociometric constructs and the techniques used to measure them. In regard to the association between acceptance and rejection, our empirical analysis confirmed the conceptual analysis of these two variables in two important ways. First, in both samples and across the two measurement techniques, they were observed to be associated in the negative linear and curvilinear ways that had been predicted. Second, the expected heterogeneity in acceptance at low levels of rejection, as well as the expected heterogeneity in rejection at the low end of acceptance, was observed, again across both samples and across measurement techniques. Together, these replications across samples and measurement procedures provide strong confirmation of the proposals we made based on a conceptual analysis of acceptance, rejection, and social preference and the associations among them.

Of equal importance to the results are the differences between the findings observed with the measures of acceptance and preference. The same pattern of *heterogeneity* in rejection was seen at the low end of both acceptance measures (the nomination and rating scale measures). And the same patterns of *homogeneity* in rejection were observed at the high and low ends of both measures of social preference (the nomination-based measure and the mean received liking-disliking score). This points to a similarity between the two acceptance scores and between the two preference scores, as well as to a difference between these two sets of scores. This pattern of findings confirms our expectation that the mean received liking-disliking rating score is a measure of social preference.

More direct evidence that the mean received rating is a measure of social preference can be seen in the comparisons of the correlation between the mean received liking-disliking rating and the nomination-based measure of acceptance, with the correlation between the mean received liking-disliking rating score and the nomination-based measure of social preference. As shown in Table 2.2, each of seven comparisons showed that the first of these correlations was significantly and substantially smaller than the second. Considered individually or together these two sets of findings confirm our assertion, derived from a conceptual analysis that the mean received liking-disliking rating score is a measure of preference and not a measure of acceptance. This finding is important, as it corrects the misleading practice seen in the literature of calling the mean received rating scale score a measure of acceptance. It is true, of course, that the mean received rating scale score is related to acceptance. Indeed it should be, simply because the construct of preference is derived in part from acceptance. Nevertheless, the mean received score is more accurately recognized as a measure of preference. These findings offer a clear answer to the second question of this study.

Just as we have shown that nomination and rating scale procedures can be used to measure the construct known as social preference, we demonstrated that both techniques can be used to index social acceptance and rejection. The two scores presumed to measure rejection revealed the same pattern of heterogeneity at low levels of acceptance and of homogeneity at high and low levels of social preference. These two scores were also highly correlated to each other, as shown in Table 2.3. In parallel to these findings, the two scores presumed to measure acceptance revealed the same pattern of heterogeneity at low levels of rejection and of homogeneity at high and low levels of social preference. These two scores were also highly correlated to each other, as shown in Table 2.4. These findings are powerful evidence of the versatility of nomination and rating scale techniques to produce measures of social preference, acceptance, and rejection.

Sociometry refers to a set of techniques as well as a way of understanding and analyzing the basic social forces among persons. We have referred to the analyses reported here as pages from a sociometric notebook. As such, they provide answers to questions about technical matters, and they contribute to an understanding of the structure of the peer group. We see here that measurement procedures are not synonymous with sociometric constructs but that different techniques can be used to measure the same phenomena. Moreover, they show the simultaneous, inextricable relatedness and independence of the concepts of acceptance and rejection. Overemphasizing their independence by treating them as separate concepts or treating them as mere opposites of each other is likely to provide equally distorted views of the dynamics that underlie children's experiences with peers. The conceptual and empirical challenges of representing the association between acceptance and rejection in theoretical and empirical models define one of the central issues of contemporary research on the peer system. A consideration of these issues will appear in further pages from our sociometric notebooks.

Notes

1. Liking and friendship are highly interrelated concepts (see Bukowski, Pizzamiglio, Newcomb, and Hoza, 1996). Studies of friendship conceptions show clearly that children see liking as a defining feature of friendship in the sense that they distinguish between the children they regard as friends and those they do not on the basis of how much they like them. Surely, children select potential friends from the pool of children whom they like the most. Whether sociometric questions that emphasize liking ("Name the girls-boys in your class you like the most") and questions that emphasize friendship ("Name the girls-boys in your class who are your friends") will produce the same results is an empirical question that to our knowledge has not received a satisfactory answer.
2. Ranking procedures had been used in sociometric assessment in the 1950s and 1960s. In these assessments children ranked all the children in the peer group according to how much they liked their peers. These assessments are no longer used.
3. Equating the variances of acceptance and rejection ensures that each is correlated with the derivative preference and impact scores to the same degree. If either acceptance or rejection had a larger variance than the other measure, then it would be more strongly associated with the measures derived from combinations of acceptance and rejection.
4. Maassen, van der Linden, Goossens, and Bokhorst (this volume) describe additional ways to derive acceptance, rejection, preference, and impact from bipolar liking ratings.

References

Asher, S. R., and Dodge, K. A. "Identifying Children Who Are Rejected by Their Peers." *Developmental Psychology,* 1986, *22,* 444–449.

Bukowski, W. M., Pizzamiglio, M. T., Newcomb, A. F., and Hoza, B. "Popularity as an Affordance for Friendship: The Link Between Group and Dyadic Experience." *Social Development,* 1996, *5,* 191–204.

Cohen, J. "Partialed Products *Are* Interactions; Partialed Powers *Are* Curve Components." *Psychological Bulletin,* 1978, *85,* 858–866.

Cohen, J., and Cohen, P. *Applied Multiple Regression/Correlation Analysis for the Behavioral Sciences.* Hillsdale, N.J.: Erlbaum, 1983.

Coie, J. D., Dodge, K. A., and Coppotelli, H. "Dimensions and Types of Social Status: A Cross-Age Perspective." *Developmental Psychology,* 1982, *18,* 557–570.

Meng, X. L., Rosenthal, R., and Rubin, D. B. "Comparing Correlated Correlation Coefficients." *Psychological Bulletin*, 1992, *111*, 172–175.

Moreno, J. L. *Who Shall Survive? A New Approach to the Problem of Human Interrelations.* Washington, D.C.: Nervous and Mental Disease Publishing Co., 1934.

Newcomb, A. F., and Bukowski, W. M. "Social Impact and Social Preference as Determinants of Children's Group Status." *Developmental Psychology*, 1983, *19*, 856–867.

Parker, J. G., and Asher, S. R. "Friendship and Friendship Quality in Middle Childhood: Links with Peer Group Acceptance and Feelings of Loneliness and Social Dissatisfaction." *Developmental Psychology*, 1993, *29*, 611–621.

WILLIAM M. BUKOWSKI is professor in the Department of Psychology of Concordia University, Montreal.

LORRIE SIPPOLA is assistant professor in the Department of Psychology of the University of Saskatchewan, Canada.

BETSY HOZA is associate professor in the Department of Psychological Sciences of Purdue University.

ANDREW F. NEWCOMB is professor in the Department of Psychology of the University of Richmond, Virginia.

3

Perceiver characteristics need to be modeled in sociometric measurement. The author accomplishes this with a latent trait model of sociometric choice that is especially successful when unlimited nominations are collected.

Recent Advances in Measurement Theory and the Use of Sociometric Techniques

Robert Terry

It is readily apparent, even to casual observers of the social sciences, that the field of sociometry has had a long and productive history. More specifically, the use of sociometric techniques in the field of peer relations to identify children who are at risk has been a productive and fruitful avenue of research (Asher, 1990).

One important and distinctive aspect of the broadly identified sociometric tradition is the explicit emphasis on measurement, the "metric" sharing equal time with the "socio." As Moreno (1946) prophetically noted, a tripartite division of emphasis exists within the research tradition into social phenomena. There are those who would stand on one foot—the "metrum." The primary focus of this division is to measure social phenomena; the kinds of social phenomena measured and their subsequent meaning are secondary. Then there are those who would stand on the other foot—the "socius." The primary focus of this group is on social relations, with measurement being essentially ignorable. Of course, implicit in this group is unconsidered measurement, as measurement begins automatically with the initial framing of the phenomena. Finally, there exist the true sociometrists who, according to Moreno, stand on both feet. For sociometrists, measurement informs theoretical understanding of social phenomena, and theoretical consideration of social phenomena informs measurement. The symbiotic relation of the "socio" and the "metric" is a quite natural and necessary evolution in the development of the scientific study of social phenomena.

In this chapter, I take the view that much of the research into sociometry via the field of peer relations has taken bifurcated paths into either the social or the metric aspect. Advances in our understanding of social phenomena and modern measurement, when mutually considered, may provide new insight and direction into reconnecting the substance with the method, bringing about sociometry in Moreno's truest sense: a science standing firmly on both feet. To that end, I present a measurement model for the typical sociometric assessment that ties current thinking on psychological measurement to current theory in social psychology regarding the process of interpersonal perception. I also present some representative data to suggest how this model is more closely tied to the empirical world than are the current sociometric models. I suggest how this merging of the "socio" and the "metric" results in the prospect of being able to answer longstanding methodological and substantive disputes in the field of peer relations. Finally, I suggest what the implications of a more modern view of measurement entail for the recent practice of sociometric measurement. The view I advance here is that, although sociometry has provided a valid and productive means of identifying at-risk individuals, further consideration of both measurement and social-psychological theories of social judgment will increase the productivity and usefulness of sociometric constructs in a variety of research enterprises.

The purpose of this chapter, then, is to reconsider the meaning of data derived via sociometric procedures from the viewpoint of modern psychometric theory. As Cronbach and Meehl (1955) would suggest, the very essence of the measurement enterprise is theory-laden, in that reconceptualizations of psychological theory are often both the cause and the effect of advances in measurement theory. I show here how such a modern view of measurement may affect the psychological theory underlying sociometric constructs. In order to frame the discussion, I first consider historical issues of measurement as they relate to the sociometric tradition.

Historical Issues in Sociometric Measurement

Sociometry was initially characterized by Moreno (1943) as a discipline defined by five important principles. The first principle suggests that sociometry is concerned with the measurement of two-way relations between entities. Although these measured relations are usually preferential in nature, this is not a necessity. Behavioral and personality assessments may be obtained via a similar technique, yet most peer relations researchers have been encouraged to view these as non-sociometric in nature (Asher and Hymel, 1981; Gronlund, 1959). Second, participants in a sociometric study must be drawn together by one or more criteria. In the field of peer relations, the commonality of school grouping procedures is typically the criterion that draws the participants into an interactive situation. Third, the measurement construct should be defined such that the participants respond with a high degree of spontaneity. This principle is designed to prevent the participants from engaging in thoughtful consideration of the sociopreferential and sociobehavioral aspects of the other participants, leading to potential socially desirable responses on the part of the participants. Fourth, the respondents should be adequately motivated so that their responses are sincere. This is intended to delimit the sociometric criteria to real-world phenomena that the sociometric participants actually care enough about to have formed prior opinions of others. Fifth, and most important, the criteria selected for testing should be, in Moreno's (1943) words, "strong, enduring, and definite; not weak, transitory, and indefinite" (p. 327). Criteria that may undergo rapid change are, in Moreno's view, of little use in determining the effects of social structure upon individuals. I comment throughout the chapter on how current sociometric practice in the peer relations field reflects Moreno's set of first principles.

Four basic methodological and measurement issues have dominated the historical literature on the foundations of sociometry. The first issue concerns stimulus-aspect differences in sociometric presentation. This issue refers to the kinds of questions that may be asked of sociometric participants. For example, "Who are your best friends?" and "Who do you like?" vary in the type of stimulus presented to the subject. The second issue concerns the effect of different methods for soliciting preference choices. An example here would contrast those who solicit ratings versus those who solicit nominations. The third issue concerns how one performs a quantitative analysis (scaling) of information provided via the sociometric test. By far the most-used method of scaling consists of summing nominations received and using some function of this score as an index of the construct of interest. Finally, the fourth issue concerns the psychometric validity of the resulting quantitative sociometric constructs. That is, what is the phenomenological meaning of a "like most" score, and how does it fit into psychological theory?

Although it may appear superficially that only the third and fourth issues are the proper dominion of measurement considerations, I show here that, consistent with Moreno's view of true sociometric practice, aspects of the first two issues interact with both quantitative analysis and validity considerations to create a total view of the "social measurement" panorama. To provide a conceptual foundation for understanding the interrelatedness of these four domains, I first discuss matters within each domain separately.

Stimulus-Aspect Differences in Sociometric Criteria

A researcher may ask a number of different questions when soliciting sociometric nominations. Generally, these can be grouped into four broad categories. *Friendship* questions such as "Who are your best friends?" or "Name your three best friends" are some of the most commonly used criteria in current sociometric practice. *Direct preference* questions such as "Name the three children that you like the most" or "like the least" are other commonly used questions. *Acquaintance* questions such as "Name all of the children that you hang around with" are used less frequently, although the use of these questions is increasing because of the blossoming interest in the construction and evaluation of peer social networks. *Task-specific choice* or *indirect preference* questions such as "Who would you like to sit next to?" or "Who would you like to play with?" are also often used, typically with the solicitation of peer ratings. This type of criterion asks participants to choose associates for a specific type of interaction.

The historical use of these different stimulus aspects reveals strengths and weaknesses in all of these criteria. Moreno (1943) strongly objected to the use of friendship, acquaintance, and direct preferential questions as criteria for true sociometric tests. In Moreno's view, the prevalent use of friendship and acquaintance criteria is "based on a misunderstanding . . . that sociometry bases its conclusions on the study of informal friendship patterns. Studies of friendship, in the literal sense, have rarely been undertaken by 'true' sociometrists, largely because friendship as a criterion is for methodological reasons undesirable. It varies in definition from individual to individual and is often a fusion of multiple criteria" (p. 326). Similarly, Moreno objected to the use of direct preference questions because, in his view, they constituted nothing more than psychological projections of "liking" reactions in undifferentiated settings.

Moreno's preference for task-specific choice questions relates to his view that choices should be more concrete than abstract, comparably meaningful, and more spontaneous than thoughtful. Because different children may use different criteria for designating friends or acquaintances, comparability in the psychological and sociological meaning of such abstract constructs as friends and acquaintances may create difficulties in constructing meaningful quantitative indices for summarizing sociometric relations. Similarly, Moreno's view that direct preference questions merely gauge psychological projections of a multidimensional construct such as liking suggests that his concern is again over the abstract nature of the question leading to potentially different ways of responding by the participants; that could possibly lead to incommensurate indices of preferential relations.

Yet the peer relations literature is saturated with the use of direct preference questions (Coie, Dodge, and Coppotelli, 1982), friendship questions (Oden and Asher, 1977; Parad, 1983), as well as task-specific choices such as playmate and workmate (Oden and Asher, 1977). Although only the latter received Moreno's ringing endorsement, I shall examine how these different stimulus-aspects and Moreno's conjectures about them fit into modern measurement models of sociometric choice.

Methods for Soliciting Sociometric Choices

A number of procedures exist for collecting sociometric choices. A substantial research base exists of studies investigating the comparability and differential validity of these methods. Characteristically, these methods of data collection are inevitably linked with certain stimulus aspects of sociometric criteria.

There are four primary methods for collecting sociometric choice information. The *peer-nomination* method asks each participant to nominate others according to a specific stimulus criterion such as friendship or liking. The *rank-order* method asks each participant to order individuals in terms of his or her own preferences on specific criteria such as friendship or liking. The *peer rating* method asks participants to rate on a Likert-type scale the extent to which others meet a specific criterion, usually liking or playmate. Finally, the method of *paired comparisons* asks the participant to make preference choices based on the presentation of all possible dyadic choices in the target sociometric group.

The research literature suggests possible strengths and weaknesses of each of these methods. The peer-nomination technique was the original suggestion of Moreno (1934). A strength of this method is the ease with which the data can be collected. The primary debate now, as then, is whether choices should be unlimited or limited, and, if limited, how many choices should be allowed (Bjerstedt, 1956). Defenders of the limited-choice (or k-choice) procedure (usually k = 3) suggest that data collection is easier, that the statistical data analysis is simplified (for the use of probability models of chance expectancy see, for example, Bronfenbrenner, 1945; Newcomb and Bukowski, 1983), and that empirical results usually show only small differences between indices derived from limited versus unlimited nominations (Bjerstedt, 1955; Gronlund, 1959; Thompson, 1960).

Proponents of the unlimited-choice procedure, including Moreno (1951), have suggested that certain artifactual constraints are placed on the data by limiting the number of choices given. Moreno (1951) argued that the transitional threshold at which nominations would cease to be given is a theoretically important construct and cannot be obtained via the limited nomination method. Furthermore, important theoretical constructs such as *social expansivity* (the tendency of participants to choose many others) and *social isolation* (the tendency of participants to receive no choices) cannot be adequately assessed with a limited-choice procedure. Finally, Holland and Leinhardt (1973) suggested that the use of a limited-nomination procedure would inevitably lead to measurement error. They gave as an example a particular voter who has exactly four best friends, all equally liked. In a circumstance where only three votes are allowed, then one best friend must be left off the list at random, leading to an increase in measurement error.

The complete rank-order procedure asks the individual to rank order, from 1 to *n* (*n* being the number of participants in the sociometric population), all sociometric participants on the criterion of interest. This is typically used only with direct and indirect preference criteria because the task of ranking all individuals on friendship and acquaintance criteria makes little sense.

The strength of this procedure is that it gives potentially more information about individual differences than does the nomination method, because of the differentiated ranking scale. This strength is offset by the empirical finding that the procedure generally leads to the inconsistent placing of participants in the middle of the distribution (Bjerstedt, 1956). Thus, voters may know their most and least favorites, but rarely do they make differentiated and ordered judgments on all individuals. This is most likely a result of unfamiliarity with all individuals in the group. As a consequence, the inability to make such differentiated choices may lead to frustration on the part of the voter and lead to less spontaneity in the choice process. Finally, it requires each voter to judge all of the other target individuals—a task that becomes excessive as the size of the sociometric population increases.

One solution to the complete rank-order method is to use a partial rank-order procedure in which individuals rank some number k at each end of the criterion and give all those in the middle a common rank. This results in a similar voting distribution based on empirical evidence but may reduce the frustration level experienced by the voters using the total-rank method. Furthermore, it does not require the voter to judge all others.

A third measurement procedure that is currently popular, in addition to the method of nominations (for example, Asher and Dodge, 1986; Ladd, 1983; Singleton and Asher, 1977), is the peer ratings method, which is quite similar to Bogardus's well-known social distance scale (1925). This method has been studied extensively and, as with all other methods, potential strengths and weaknesses have been identified. The complete peer ratings method, like the complete ranking method, has the potential for providing more discriminating information. The method also makes for a more subtle transition to rejection reports. Yet, unlike the total rankings method, it does not force voters to make differentiated rankings of individuals for whom their judgments are the same. In other words, it simultaneously limits the number of ranking possibilities (for example, 1–5) while permitting ties.

The disadvantages are both pragmatic and theoretical. Pragmatically, the complete-rating method requires a great deal more time than does the nomination method. The task may also be frustrating to voters because of the task demand of rating all peers, leading to less spontaneous judgments. It has also been demonstrated that ratings do not permit the identification of socially isolated individuals (Terry and Coie, 1991). Finally, it is well known that substantial response-set tendencies may exist for any assessment situation (Jackson, 1972). If this is the case, the scoring of ratings must incorporate the possibility of different rater response-set tendencies (Terry and Coie, 1991).

Finally, the method of paired comparisons is used infrequently in current research. Although it has been argued that this method might be superior because it makes each voter's comparative judgments explicit (Guilford, 1954), judging all possible pairs of peers is an excessive task (Bjerstedt, 1956). For example, there are 276 paired comparisons for a small population of twenty-five persons, excluding comparisons involving the voter. One way to reduce the task is to *sample* from the set of all possible pairs, but little research into this possibility has been conducted.

The common ancestry of the nomination, ranking, and rating methods can be recognized by viewing them as an ordered hierarchy. The complete-ranking method is the most general because it allows for $n - 1$ distinctions among those in the population. The partial-ranking method is a subset, in that a voter ranks up to k-choices (k may be fixed or unlimited) at both ends of the criterion, and gives all those judged to be in the middle of the criterion the same tied value, allowing for a minimum of $1 + 2k$ and a maximum of $n - 1$ scale values per voter. The complete-ratings method further restricts the partial-ranking method by limiting the number of acceptable scale values given (say k) and allowing tied ranks for any of the k-scale values. Hence, the number of observed scale values for the total-ratings method is k. Typically, this is operationalized as a 1–5 Likert-type scale. Finally, the nomination method is a subset of the ratings method, in that k is restricted to k = 2 values: a votee is either nominated or not nominated. Within the nomination method, one can further subset the methods into limited (partial nomination) versus unlimited nominations.

Because of the hierarchical relationship of these methods, the *potential* for gathering more information from voters with respect to individual differences in the criterion varies from a potential low via the nomination method to a potential high via the total-ranking method. As we shall see, the actual realization of this differential potential may not be empirically obtainable. Because the methods of paired comparisons, complete rankings, and partial rankings are not commonly used in current sociometric research, further discussion of them will be limited.

Quantitative Analysis of Sociometric Information

Once the pairing of stimulus-aspect with a method of soliciting sociometric choices has been made, the next step is to apply some method to quantify the data. Usually, this consists of the condensation of the choice data into a numerical index for each individual that gives meaning to the nature of the social phenomena under study.

In this regard, two major avenues of research have coexisted since Moreno's time. The first, centered around the *group-directed* nature of the phenomena, seeks to develop indices for structural components of the group, with "group" as the unit of analysis. More commonly known as *social network* analysis, indices such as network density, group cohesion, and group egalitarianism are determined (Scott, 1991). The group-directed approach also includes methods to determine subgroups and cliques (Iacobucci, 1990; Kindermann, 1998).

The second research avenue, aptly termed as having an *individual-directed* focus, attempts to characterize the relationship of the individual to the group. Such indices as social acceptance and rejection, social status, social isolation, and social visibility are derived to examine the nature of the individual and his or her role in the social group. In this chapter, I focus on the individual as the unit of analysis.

Social acceptance is usually determined by adding the number of positive nominations ("like most") received by individuals and denoting those with high scores as socially accepted. *Social rejection* is usually defined by adding the number of negative nominations ("like least") received and denoting those with high scores as socially rejected. When using the complete ratings method, it is typically the case that those with the *highest average* rating are deemed the most socially accepted, whereas those with the *lowest average* rating are deemed the most socially rejected. In either case, the indices derived from nominations or ratings involve simple sums or averages of evaluations received.

Social neglect has typically been determined by adding the number of votes received by an individual; those with very few votes (Coie and Dodge, 1983) or no votes at all (Terry and Coie, 1991; Williams and Asher, 1987) are defined as social isolates. The criteria over which these votes are summed may vary; it may be over both positive and negative criteria (for example, "like most" and "like least"), or limited to "like most" only. One criticism of the ratings method is that it does not provide an index that is the logical equivalent to the sum of positive and negative nominations. However, Asher and Dodge (1986) combined the positive nomination method ("like most") with the complete ratings method to produce an algorithm for estimating social isolation.

Likewise, an index for *social visibility* or *social impact* has been defined by adding the number of votes received by an individual on both positive and negative dimensions and denoting those with high scores as being highly visible players in the social group (Coie and others, 1982). Although the term *social impact* was originally used to label this index, I prefer the term *social visibility*, which has less the connotation of active engagement with others on the part of the "socially impactive" person and more the connotation of joint engagement between perceivers and the "socially visible" individuals. Regardless of terminology, this index serves to indicate those individuals who elicit strong opinions in their peers. Like social neglect or isolation, the method of total ratings does not logically provide a mechanism to estimate social visibility. However, Asher and Dodge (1986) have again suggested a method for combining positive nominations and ratings to approximate a social visibility score.

Indices of *social status* have been developed in an attempt to classify individuals into homogeneous categories that describe the role of the individual in the group (Terry and Coie, 1991). These include such labels as popular, rejected, controversial, neglected, and average. These classifications have generally involved an attempt to identify relatively dense clusters in the two-dimensional space defined by the uncorrelated dimensions of social preference and social impact. As such, different classification systems will result of two primary factors: (1) type of classification method used and (2) initial derivation of the social preference and social impact dimensions. In this chapter the latter issue is of concern.

There are numerous other indices, but in the interest of brevity I will not discuss them here. One exception is the concept of *reciprocated friendships* (for example, Bukowski and Hoza, 1989; Price and Ladd, 1986). The computation of this index typically requires a sociometric criterion specifically about friendship and is almost always collected via nominations. The index is defined by counting the number of friendship nominations given by a voter that are reciprocated by the votees. The number of reciprocated nominations may then be used as an index of the quantity of social support that the person (voter) receives. (I discuss the importance of reciprocated nominations for non-friendship questions later.)

One curious shortcoming of the statistical indices developed to capture the group-individual relationship is the lack of quantitative measures for the underlying processes that voters use to make their choices. If Moreno's (1943) commandment about the two-way nature of sociometric data is correct, a focus only on votes received ignores crucial information contained in the pattern of choices made by the voters. In a later section, I propose a comprehensive model that integrates choices received and given in a psychologically meaningful framework.

Psychometric Validity Research

Historically, sociometric research has been used with some success to guide researchers in their choice of an appropriate methodology. Perhaps the most crucial and most often addressed questions concern (1) aspect differences in the criterion (for example, direct preferential versus friendship criteria), (2) use of ratings versus nominations, (3) use of limited versus unlimited nominations, and (4) number of optimal choices when using limited nominations. One other crucial aspect that has been studied but will not be examined here is methods for classifying children into status groups (Terry and Coie, 1991).

Even in a chapter devoted to sociometric methodology, a complete review of the empirical literature on the operating characteristics of various sociometric methodologies is impossible. Instead, it is more fruitful to focus on the guiding themes of such research and ask whether or not the psychometric dimensions on which such comparisons are made are reasonable and complete from the point of view of modern measurement theory.

To assess the comparative psychometric validity of different sociometric methods, two time-honored psychometric principles have been followed. Following Cronbach and Meehl's (1955) recommendation, two important aspects of classical measurement theory—*reliability* of measurement and *construct validity*—have served as the holy grails of sociometric research. To the extent that it showed comparatively better reliability and more consistent nomothetic relations with other externally valid constructs, a method was seen as more valid psychometrically. However, as I show later, additional psychometric considerations play a role in determining the adequacy and usefulness of competing sociometric technologies.

To gauge the reliability of sociometric measurement, researchers have relied on test-retest reliability, as indexed by the short-term stability of sociometric scores. Use of this gauge implicitly presumes that a person's social standing is of a trait-like nature, such that in the short-term, "true" individual change in the construct is not likely to occur (Anastasi, 1988). The typical interval that has been used to assess stability has ranged from three months to two years (Gronlund, 1959; Mouton, Blake, and Fruchter, 1955).

Use of the test-retest correlation has not been without its detractors, however. A number of methodologists have noted potential shortcomings of the test-retest methodology to estimate measurement reliability. Generally, a test-retest correlation is a useful measure of consistent, reliable measurement *only* under the strong assumption that no systematic changes in the construct have occurred over the test-retest interval. This assumption is in concert with Moreno's suggestion that sociometric criteria should be strong, enduring, and definite. If so, short-term stability coefficients are acceptable indicators of the consistency of measurement.

However, if systematic changes do occur in the sociometric construct, then what is actually assessed is the stability of the characteristic rather than the reliability of the measurement. Thus, the use of test-retest correlations may confound systematic and nonsystematic change in ways that cannot speak to the precision of measurement. Pepinsky (1949) and Harmon (1949) noted the problematic nature of assessing consistency of measurement when conceptualizing sociometric measurement within a classical psychometric framework. However, Bjerstedt (1956) suggested that stability correlations can be valid indices of the consistency of sociometric measurement. He argued that, even though instability may be more a function of real change than measurement error, the necessity of high stability in preferential constructs is of utmost importance if such a construct is to be of predictive utility. Bjerstedt also pointed out that it was crucial to obtain an estimate of the true stability of a preferential score, avoiding estimating spurious instability (instability in the observed scores in spite of actual stability in the true scores) and spurious stability (stability in observed scores in spite of actual instability in the true scores). In both of these situations, it is well known (Lord and Novick, 1968) that achieving an unbiased estimate of the true stability requires some knowledge of the reliability of the observed scores.

Although the concept of internal consistency as a psychometric gauge existed at the time, sociometrists rarely used it to evaluate the consistency of measurement due to theoretical objections. Pepinsky (1949) argued that psychometric measurement differed from sociometric measurement *in prin-*

ciple because psychometric scales expect some degree of consensus among replicable indicators of a construct, yet no such consensus among voters in sociometric choices is expected. Suffice it to say that such a principle is a matter for empirical investigation, and whether such an assumption is justifiable will be examined later.

I will not discuss construct validity research on the place of sociometric indicators in a nomothetic network. It is sufficient to acknowledge that sociometric indicators have played a central role in understanding psychological and sociological phenomena (Asher, 1990). Yet we should be reminded that measurement imprecision may still play a crucial role in this valuable enterprise by attenuating the quantitative estimates of the nomothetic links. It is my position that such attenuation has usually occurred, and I present examples.

How Should We Evaluate Sociometric Methodology?

Modern measurement theory, via such conceptual models as item response theory (IRT), has developed a set of psychometric criteria that are broader in scope than those defined by reliability and nomothetic span. The extent to which a measure meets these broader criteria is an indication of the meaningfulness of the measurement paradigm and the resulting numerical assignments. Briefly, the most important of these criteria include (1) the notion of the *dimensionality* of a test construct, (2) the use of *optimal scaling* methods for assigning quantitative indices, and (3) modeling the measurement process to reflect *construct representativeness* (Embretson, 1983).

The importance of assessing the dimensionality of a construct cannot be overstated. Test theorists generally agree that meaningful statements about a construct cannot exist unless it is unidimensional (Anderson and Gerbing, 1982; Hattie, 1985; Thissen, Steinberg, Pyszczynski, and Greenberg, 1983). If unidimensionality does not exist, individual differences in the measured construct reflect a mixture of multiple criteria, and the construct is rendered less interpretable. For example, the simple sum of nominations or the averaged obtained peer rating to index social acceptance fails the unidimensionality criterion because the obtained construct reflects the multiple and diverse meaning systems used by each of the voters in making their sociometric choices. The importance of the unidimensionality assumption was recognized early (Moreno, 1943; Northway, 1946; Bjerstedt, 1956) but not further investigated.

The notion of *optimal scaling* has had a long and vigorous history in both psychometry and sociometry. Simply put, the idea is that, under the assumption of unidimensionality, some weighted combination of the data might provide more precise measurement than a simple sum or average of the data (Bjerstedt, 1956; Lord and Novick, 1968). In the sociometric literature, various weighting schemes have been tried (Gronlund, 1955). The basic conclusion of the sociometric literature is that the simplest weighting schemes generally worked about as well as the more complicated ones. One shortcoming of this work, however, is that the weighting schemes were heuristically derived. As such, the weights were not determined in such a way as to maximize the efficiency of the resulting score with respect to any substantive model. Current psychometric methods such as IRT-based measurement do suggest model-based optimal weighting schemes and imply that a corresponding increase in efficiency may be gained by using such a model-based framework (Birnbaum, 1968). I shall later show how such weights can be used to create more efficient, precise measurement of sociometric constructs.

Finally, Embretson (1983) suggested that an overlooked component of the construct validation process is the notion of *construct representation*. This component is concerned with identifying the theoretical mechanisms that underlie the observed responses, or model validity. All things being equal, constructs with theoretically meaningful representations are preferred to constructs with less meaningful representations.

Sociometry as a discipline has primarily focused on establishing the breadth of the nomothetic network in establishing construct validity. Underlying most sociometric constructs, however, are implicit models that make certain assumptions about the nature of the phenomenon as it is captured. To clarify this idea, I now present a model that I believe captures the latent mechanisms underlying observed sociometric choices within a peer group.

A Latent Model of Sociometric Choice

Northway (1946) suggested that the assumptions and methods of sociometry were fundamentally psychological rather than sociological. These assumptions centered around the process of one individual choosing one or more persons among many on a defined criterion of interest—a psychological problem roughly comparable to the interest of psychophysics in the ability of the individual to discriminate among many objects. In sociometry, then, I submit that the substantive issue is one of interpersonal perception and social judgment: How does one person regard another person in the context of others? To properly understand the meaning of sociometric choice is to properly understand the process by which one person perceives the nature of another on some social criterion.

To adequately capture the spirit of the perceptual-judgment process, a model needs to be complex enough to reproduce the observed data, contain enough parameters to capture both voter and votee characteristics, and be mathematical-statistical in nature so as to ensure reproducibility across investigators. With this in mind, I propose that a useful model for understanding the process of making social judgments is the latent trait model of interpersonal perception (LaTRIPP). The model proposes that we consider the *probability that person i receives a vote from voter j* (denoted as π_{ij}) as a function of three model parameters: θ_i the level of the trait "possessed" by votee i; β_j, the social sensitivity of voter j to the criterion θ; and, β_j, the social threshold of voter (j) to the criterion θ. The general idea, then, is to model the process by which some votee (i) receives a nomination from some voter (j) on some latent criterion of interest (trait). The parameters of the model are related by the following equation:

$$(1)\ \pi_{ij} = \{\ 1 + \exp\ [\ -1.7\ \alpha_j\ (\theta_i - \beta j)\ ]\ \}^{\ -1}$$

This equation describes a simple logistic curve denoting the nonlinear regression of the parameter θ_{ij} on the trait parameter α_i, with the α_i and the β_j serving as the regression slope and threshold, respectively. Figure 3.1 contains one such curve for a voter (j) with a social sensitivity parameter α_j equal to 0.8, and a social threshold parameter β_j equal to 1.0.

The substantive interpretation of the social sensitivity and social threshold models are crucial in evaluating the psychological plausibility of the model. What gives this model important psychological meaning is the interpretation of the parameters as social psychological variables central to the process of interpersonal perception. Thus, the propensity of receiving a nomination is a function of the level of the attribute θ residing in the person being judged, the judge's social threshold for responding to varying levels of the attribute, and the social sensitivity of the judge in being able to discriminate between persons with varying degrees of the attribute. The social threshold parameter (a property of the voter) is roughly analogous to the propensity of the voter to give many or few nominations. For example, a voter who gives many nominations on "like most" would have a low threshold for giving a positive judgment for liking to others; voters who give few "like most" nominations to others have high thresholds for giving positive nominations.

The social sensitivity parameter (also a property of the judge) is roughly analogous to the ability of the voter to make discriminations among the pool of votees. In the field of social perception, this parameter corresponds directly to the identification of a voter as a "good judge" of individuals. As Figure 3.1

Figure 3.1. Person Perception Function with $\alpha = 0.8$ and $\beta = 1.0$

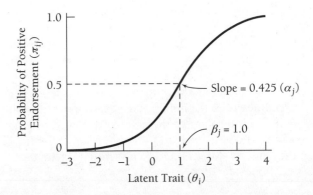

suggests, this parameter is operationally defined to be proportional to the slope of the curve. Thus, voters with a social sensitivity parameter of zero on the "like most" criterion would be depicted as showing a flat, horizontal line. This would indicate that this particular voter would be a poor judge because his or her vote would not vary with individual differences in likability.

This model is also interesting in that it postulates only a single-dimensioned attribute (θ) to account for the various voter-votee response patterns. As discussed further in Terry (1999), I have suggested that this model is in close agreement with Kelley's (1967) theory of social attribution. In this theory, Kelley suggested that attributions about objects are consistent with a dispositional view of the behavior of the object if the twin concepts of consensus and distinctiveness are met. For social attribution, this implies that the social perceptions of the persons in the group are consistent with a perceptual model of dispositional attribution if (1) the perceivers achieve consensus in their view of the social attributes of the perceived objects, and (2) the perceivers are able to discriminate between the various perceived objects on the social attribute of interest. The consensus requirement is essentially modeled as an assumption (though testable) of a unidimensional trait; that is, all judges are responding systematically to individual differences along a single trait dimension. The "distinctiveness" requirement of Kelley's theory is conveniently located in the LaTRIPP model in terms of the α_j parameter, which is presumed to be non-zero for all (or at worst, most) voters. It remains, of course, to be determined whether the model as formulated is consistent with empirical data.

When the social sensitivity parameter α_j is presumed to be invariant across judges (that is, $\alpha = _j$ for all j), the model reduces to a simplified form known as the Rasch model (Rasch, 1966). This model has certain desirable features; most important, a simple sum or average of the choices received would capture all of the available information in the data, resulting in an optimally efficient score. For this condition to hold, however, all judges would need to be equally perceptive to the criterion stimulus. Observation of humans making social judgments suggests that this assumption is generally unrealistic. As I shall show, an IRT framework using the LaTRIPP model provides a statistically sound way to test this conjecture.

What gives this model usefulness for statistical and measurement purposes is the fact that it is a specific case of the general two-parameter (or Birnbaum) IRT model. Because the statistical properties of this model have been heavily researched, a well-understood framework exists for considering the implications of the model for substantive questions (see Thissen and Steinberg, 1988). Furthermore, the thorny statistical issues of obtaining estimates for the parameters of the model and assessing the fit of the model to empirical data have been solved to the point that such substantive research can proceed (Bock and Aitken, 1981). The programs PC-BILOG (Mislevy and Bock, 1990) and PC-MULTILOG (Thissen, 1991) are useful in fitting the models under consideration.

Terry (1999) discusses in greater detail the statistical issues involved in fitting the LaTRIPP model to sociometric data obtained via the standard nomination technique. Suffice it to say that the model considers the *voter's response pattern* in estimating the parameters of the model. This notion is in concert with Bjerstedt's (1956) prescient conceptualization that a successful science of sociometry would not just consider the number of choices received as indicative of social status but would expand consideration to *who* actually made the choices. We can now say that, forty years later, Bjerstedt's prescience has finally been validated.

Implications of the Model: An Empirical Example

To understand the implications of the LaTRIPP model as a conceptual basis for establishing meaning in sociometric measurement, I discuss a representative subset of the data presented in Terry (1999) to fully demonstrate the explanatory power of the model. The data presented come from a single eighth-grade school on which sociometric nominations were solicited from 102 judges on 121 persons. The data were collected on eleven criteria in all; only the standard sociometric criteria of likability (those you like most), unlikability (those you like least), and popularity (those who most others like) are reported here. All stimuli were of a direct preferential nature. Data were collected in such a way that both limited ($k = 3$) and unlimited choice measurements were obtained. This permitted the direct comparison of the two methods of soliciting nominations in terms of implications about the model parameters and overall model fit.

The data were preprocessed via a set of SAS macros (Terry, 1995) for analysis via the PC-BILOG program. Once the model has been fit, we can use the various statistical tools provided by the IRT framework to assist us in answering certain unresolved methodological issues concerning sociometric measurement. I turn to such questions now.

Distributional Nature of the Data. It has long been suggested by sociometric researchers that limiting the number of nominations to some small number, usually three, is adequate because voters rarely nominate more than a small number of individuals on sociometric criteria (see Thompson, 1960). Yet the possibility remains that this empirical finding is an artifact. One possible explanation is the use of friendship stimuli rather than direct preference stimuli. Whereas the number of one's friends may be small, a greater number of choices may be given in response to a direct preference question such as liking.

Second, the method of recording of sociometric choices can limit the number of choices given. For example, writing down the names of one's choices is time consuming and may artifactually reduce the number of choices because of fatigue and frustration with this task. Because our judges only had to place a mark next to the names of their choices, we reduced, if not eliminated, the fatigue and frustration element. This procedure also

Table 3.1. Descriptive Statistics for Nominations Received on Three Sociometric Items for Limited-Choice and Unlimited-Choice Methods

Item	Liked Most		Liked Least		Liked by Most Others	
Method	Limited Choice	Unlimited Choice	Limited Choice	Unlimited Choice	Limited Choice	Unlimited Choice
Statistic						
Mean	2.7	35.1	2.0	16.6	1.5	13.4
Standard Deviation	2.7	15.1	3.0	9.4	2.8	8.5
Range	15.0	62.0	16.0	42.0	18.0	40.0
Quartile Range	3.0	22.0	2.0	11.0	2.0	12.0
Skewness	1.6	− 0.2	2.0	1.3	3.4	0.8
Kurtosis	3.9	− 0.9	4.6	1.3	13.9	0.4

better accommodates Moreno's principle that sociometric choices should be spontaneous and unreflected.

Table 3.1 presents summary statistics of the raw number of votes received for both fixed and unlimited methods. It is clear that a much greater range of values is obtained when using the unlimited-choice method. The result of using a limited-choice method is an artificial constraint on the distribution of choices received; the data are quite skewed and clumped near a value less than 3 on all three criteria. Use of normal theory statistical methods such as regression or path analysis on the usual criterion of summing votes received will not be entirely justifiable when using the limited-choice method; the skewness and kurtosis values deviate quite a bit from their desired value of zero.

By comparison, the unlimited-choice method results in a much greater range of values on all three criteria. We have minimally doubled the range of votes received while creating a distribution of votes received that is much more consonant with normality, as seen in the obtained values of skewness and kurtosis. The mean number of votes received for the unlimited-choice method is minimally six times the mean number of votes received for the limited-choice method, and the interquartile range is minimally four times greater when using an unlimited-choice procedure.

All things considered, the use of unlimited-choice methods has resulted in a set of data that have more desirable distributional properties than a set of data gleaned from a limited-choice method. Although this is an important methodological finding, I now show how an application of the LaTRIPP model to these data results in a construct with superior measurement properties.

Assessing Model Fit. We used the software package PC-BILOG (Mislevy and Bock, 1990) to estimate the parameters of the model and to assess the fit of the model to the data. Details on the fitting of the model to sociometric data are contained in Terry (1999).

It is common in fitting IRT-type models to real data to begin with the simplest model possible and expand the complexity of the model according to the empirical demands of the data. If the data happen to coincide with the simplest models, then the model-fitting exercise ends early in the process.

With this in mind, we first compared the fit of the equal social sensitivity (Rasch) model to a model (LaTRIPP) that allowed "judge sensitivity" parameters to vary over judges. For each model, a -2 log-likelihood G^2 value is calculated, which reflects the degree of lack of fit of the model to the data. Because the Rasch model is nested within the more general LaTRIPP model, we can statistically compare the differential fit of two models via a χ^2 difference test (known generally as a difference in likelihood ratio test (DLRT; Mislevy and Bock, 1990). For example, $G^2 = 11,786.52$ for the Rasch model when fit to the "like most" question, and $G^2 = 11,225.05$ when fit to the LaTRIPP model. The difference is given as DLRT = 561.47, based on 102 degrees of freedom (the number of voters). This difference is statistically significant at $p = .001$, suggesting that the more complicated two-parameter model is preferred to the simpler Rasch model. In psychological terms, this means that all judges are *not* alike; that is, some voters are better judges of who is more or less likeable. As I later suggest, this important finding has important methodological and statistical implications for gathering and scoring sociometric data.

The other items showed similar findings. DLRT values of 308.34 and 409.21 were obtained for the "like least" and "liked by most others" questions, respectively. Both were statistically significant as well (df = 102). Thus, the findings indicated that judges do differ in their sensitivity to social preferential criteria. The model suggests clearly that in order to understand the meaning of sociometric constructs, the researcher must consider the social-psychological processes used when making social choices.

Of course, the fact that the two-parameter model fits better in a statistical sense than the one-parameter model does not imply that the LaTRIPP model fits the data very well at a global level. That is, it is quite possible that neither model would adequately account for the observed data. The assessment of model fit at the global level goes directly to the issue of the unidimensionality of the construct. If the model fails, then the most likely explanation is that the process of making sociometric choices is multidimensional in nature. If so, the model would imply a lack of consensus when making sociometric choices, contraindicating the validity of Kelley's criteria concerning dispositional attribution.

To assess global model fit, we used a heuristic index developed by Mislevey and Bock (1990). This index is based on the likelihood-ratio, chi-square statistic G^2 that is obtained by comparing the proportion of observed nominations within a small interval of θ with the proportion expected based on fitting the model. Like most χ^2-like indices, the greater the correspondence between observed (ρ_{ij}) and expected (estimated [π_{ij}] from the model) frequencies, the better the fit of the model. It has been suggested that for descriptive purposes, the ratio of G^2 to its degrees of freedom provides a more interpretable index than a simple value. This fit ratio should be near 1 for well-fitting models and certainly less than 3 for good-fitting models (Anderson and Gerbing, 1988; Baker, 1992; Wheaton, Muthen, Alwin, and Summers, 1977). In the event that this global fit statistic fails to meet our criterion for good fit, then we would have to reject the model as a whole.

The results indicated that the LaTRIPP model strongly fits the data for all three criteria. We obtained fit-ratio values of 1.02, 1.01, and 1.37 for the "like most," "like least," and "liked by most others" criteria, respectively. It appears that the model is justified for use with sociometric data because it reproduces the observed nomination patterns quite well. Substantively, the inability to reject the unidimensional assumption provides strong evidence that the process of social perception operating in the making of sociometric choices is consistent with Kelley's (1967) theory of dispositional attribution, where the "consensus" criterion is considered isomorphic with the assumption of trait unidimensionality.

For completeness, I also fit the full LaTRIPP model to data obtained via the limited-choice method. The fit ratios were 2.43, 4.55, and 35.35 for "like most," "like least," and "liked by most others," respectively. Not surprisingly, these are worse than those obtained when using the unlimited-choice method. In the context of a model of interpersonal perception, the restrictiveness of the limited-choice method results in a limitation of the ability to fully account for the observed data via person-specific perceptual parameters.

These data also allow us to reflect on one important point: the relative goodness-of-fit between minimally acceptable models that is crucial to our understanding of the process. It is clear that assessing "like most" with a limited-choice option provides a minimally acceptable model by our global goodness-of-fit criterion. Yet we see that the fit statistics for "like most" using unlimited nominations is clearly superior to those obtained using limited choices. So my conclusion is that although either method falls into the minimally acceptable range, the use of unlimited choices provides for a superior model fit to the data.

Social Sensitivity and the Concept of Information

An important statistical concept emanating from the framework of IRT is the concept of *information* (Birnbaum, 1968; Hambleton and Swaminathan, 1985). Information is an important concept in IRT because it relates directly to the notion that more available information leads to a reduction in uncertainty. In this scenario, I suggest that the more information we obtain, the more certain we can be about each person's sociometric standing. To that end, the concept of information in IRT is directly related to the important measurement concept of *precision of measurement*. Essentially, the greater the precision of measurement, the more *information* contained in the measurement. Thus, information and precision, as reflected in the standard error of measurement, are directly related and reflect the degree of uncertainty in any given measurement.

The importance of this concept is rooted in the fact that we can estimate an *information function* (IF) for each judge, and by summing up each of the judge's individual information functions, obtain a *group information function* (GIF) reflecting measurement uncertainty for the entire sociometric procedure. Each judge's IF reflects, over the entire range of θ values, the degree to which that person is a "good" or "bad" judge, relative to group consensus on the unidimensional attribute θ. It follows that the GIF reflects the total information provided by the sociometric procedure in estimating attribute scores. We note that, in general, the information function is not uniform over the range of θ. That is, individuals will be more perceptive over certain ranges of θ than over others. This property will also be true for the GIF. Further details on the information function in IRT can be found in Birnbaum (1968) and for this case specifically in Terry (1999).

Interestingly, the information provided by an individual judge is proportionally related to her social sensitivity. The psychological meaning of this statistical fact is straightforward: *judges are more informative when they are more socially sensitive or perceptive.* Whereas judges with high α's are precise, judges with low α's are imprecise in their judgments (regarding the social consensus). This notion of sensitivity to the social consensus follows directly from the assumption of unidimensionality of the construct; however, it is a testable assumption that was in fact consistent with the data. Given the verity of this assumption, the social sensitivity parameter is directly interpretable as the degree of sensitivity to the group consensus.

We can now examine the extent to which judges vary in their social sensitivity to group norms. We have shown by comparing the two-parameter model (α_j varying) with the Rasch model (α_j = for all j) that social sensitivity among judges does indeed vary. Table 3.2 reports descriptive data on the estimated sensitivity parameters for both limited and unlimited-choice methods. It is clear that the estimated values of the sensitivity parameter vary across judges; it is also clear that the mean of the sensitivity indices are suppressed and the range of values is restricted for the fixed-choice procedure when compared to the unlimited-choice procedure. Because the values of the sensitivity parameter are directly related to information and precision of measurement, the results show that the limited-choice method places artifactual constraints on the measurement process, resulting in less precise measurement, as foretold by Moreno (1951).

A more direct comparison of the measurement efficiency of the unlimited- and limited-choice procedures is to compare their group information functions (GIFs). The ratio of the information functions of two procedures is an index of the relative efficiency (Lord, 1980). Because the GIFs

Table 3.2. Descriptive Data on Estimated Social Sensitivity Parameters (Slopes)

Statistic	Mean of Estimated Slopes		Standard Deviation of Estimated Slopes		Interquartile Range of Estimated Slopes	
Method	Limited Choice	Unlimited Choice	Limited Choice	Unlimited Choice	Limited Choice	Unlimited Choice
Item						
Like Most	0.31	0.61	0.20	0.34	[.23, .36]	[.36, .77]
Like Least	0.34	0.44	0.22	0.20	[.03, .48]	[.32, .53]
Liked by						
Most Others	0.33	0.67	0.20	0.22	[.03, .59]	[.41, .89]

are not uniformly constant over θ, I computed the *average* (over θ) amount of group information obtained for each procedure and then computed the relative efficiency ratio for these averages. The results indicate that using the LaTRIPP model on unlimited-choice data provides a 2,770 percent increase in efficiency over computing a simple sum score on limited-choice data. In other words, the estimated θ scores derived from applying the model to unlimited-choice data are 27.7 times more efficient (precise) than the usual sum scores derived from standard sociometric analysis of limited-choice data. As Lord (1980) noted, this is equivalent to needing 27.7 times more judges to reach the same level of measurement precision.

Deriving Scale Scores

The most common method of deriving estimated trait (attribute) scores from sociometric nomination procedures is to simply sum or average the votes received from all judges. In the previous discussion, I suggested that a simple sum score may not be the most efficient way to compute these scores. In fact, Birnbaum (1968) demonstrated mathematically that, given a two-parameter model, the simple sum score is neither an efficient nor a sufficient estimator of the trait parameter θ. That is, using a simple sum of the choices received as an estimator for the trait θ does *not* use all of the available information contained in the data and is therefore not sufficient. Accordingly, use of the simple sum score results in less precision of measurement, making it an inefficient index. Birnbaum does suggest, however, that a suitably *weighted* sum will be optimal in the sense of using all of the available information. By now, it should come as no surprise that these weights are simply the social sensitivity parameters (α_j). *Each choice received should be weighted by the social sensitivity of the person who gave the nomination.*

A simple example will make this clear. Suppose that an individual voter, upon making sociometric choices, makes them entirely at random with respect to the criterion of interest. Clearly, such a voter would obtain little if any degree of social consensus with any other voter by the simple fact that such an individual's pattern of votes would of necessity be uncorrelated with any other pattern of votes. Any attempt to include such an individual's nominations into the scoring algorithm can only add error to the ultimate index. Of course, rarely will such random patterns exist. More likely, some judges are simply not finely attuned to the social group, and thus their judgments correlate poorly with others' judgments. By the same argument, these votes should be weighted less heavily than others, with the weights depending on their degree of sensitivity.

This suggests the importance of considering the pattern of votes received rather than the simple quantity of votes received. This is sensible both statistically and substantively, in that we obtain more precise estimates of trait levels when we give greater weight to those judges most perceptive for the trait. For example, a person choosing others randomly would obtain $\alpha_j = 0$; because the person is completely insensitive to the dimension being judged, any choice received from that person would not (and should not) count at all in estimating any one person's trait score. Clearly, then, the LaTRIPP model suggests some potentially useful ways for reducing measurement error that are consistent with the substantively important social-psychological principles underlying the processes of interpersonal perception and social attribution.

Conclusions and Future Directions

The purpose of this chapter was to critically examine the basic methodological and statistical considerations of the sociometric method from the point of view of modern measurement theory. An additional goal was to develop a better model for sociometric data that addresses persistent, seemingly intractable methodological questions. Consequently, a new model—LaTRIPP—for the social-psychological task of making sociometric choices was developed. This model demonstrated (1) the superiority of unlimited over limited nominations, (2) the superiority of optimally quantified indices over simple sum scores, (3) that sociometric choices conform to a unidimensional trait model with direct preference stimuli, which indicates a common perceptual framework for the group, and (4) individuals making sociometric choices vary in their sensitivity to group norms.

The model also provides solutions for other pervasive methodological issues. A common debate regards the use of direct preference ("like most") versus friendship questions. I suggest that friendship as a measure of *social acceptance* is not a unidimensionally scalable stimulus. Based on psychological theories of friendship formation, I predict that choices of friends would not adequately fit a unidimensional model of choice. If this is true, one can argue (as Moreno did) that any criterion score resulting from a summing of nominations is an unacceptable fusion of multiple criteria, yielding a psychological construct devoid of meaning; any attempt to summarize such data in a single index is potentially misleading. In the vernacular, such a practice constitutes the comparing of apples and oranges. If this prediction can be empirically validated, the use of friendship nominations rather than likability nominations may be responsible for findings that suggest reduced stability in "social acceptance" across situations and occasions (see Wright, Giammarino, and Parad, 1986). Undoubtedly, a different social-psychological model operates when nominations are solicited via a friendship stimulus. This is inconsistent with Moreno's principle that the criteria should be relatively enduring, or trait-like, in nature. Moreno argued strongly that friendship did not meet this principle and was thus not properly sociometric in nature.

The preceding argument does not, however, imply that there is no observable relation between friendship and liking. We might expect that most people like their friends, so there will be some overlap of the two criteria. But the two concepts are not symmetric and fungible. It is quite reasonable to expect that highly likable individuals will have a greater likelihood of acquiring more friends. Yet liking is only one of the many bases for engaging in a friendship relation. One could acquire particular friendships for a number of different reasons unrelated to liking. For example, a friendship may result from propinquity, similarity, a fundamental lack of available alternatives (no one else will be your friend), matched instrumentality (each person serving the needs of the other to create a greater whole), and for other reasons in which liking is not the precipitating factor. Likewise, a highly likable person may choose to not engage in many specific friendships. Thus, although liking and friendship are related in any given social group, they are not interchangeable.

A second ongoing debate appears to concern the comparative profitably of using roster-and-rating sociometric techniques over standard nomination techniques. Michelson and Wood (1980) suggested that rating scales result in greater range, variability, and a more normal-like distribution in scores than do nomination (limited) methods. Of course, we have seen that using unlimited nominations results in superior distributional properties also. Parker, Rubin, Price, and DeRosier (1995) suggested that rating scale scores may have more attractive scaling properties than simple tallies of choices. This *may* be true *if* the nominations are limited in nature *and* if the choices are not optimally weighted by the individual judge's sensitivity to the group consensus. However, I have shown that using unlimited nominations with direct preference questions in combination with the optimal scaling features provided by the LaTRIPP paradigm meet the desirable scaling properties of unidimensionality and optimally efficient measurement, and further satisfy the construct representativeness criterion advocated by Embretson (1983). It may also occur to the thoughtful reader that ratings are similarly susceptible to the problems of differential social sensitivity and social expansivity. One may also note that ratings should be assessed for unidimensionality;

recall that in the absence of unidimensional measurement, no single index can be formed that has an unambiguous interpretation. Fortunately, one can extend the LaTRIPP model to handle data that are ordinal rather than nominal in nature by using *graded IRT models* (Thissen and Steinberg, 1988). This entails no special difficulties and provides the interested sociometrician with a framework for assessing the unidimensionality assumption, constructing group information curves, and obtaining optimally weighted scores. An interesting study would be to compare the information curves for both the nomination and rating scale methods in order to assess the relative efficiency of the two methods.

Finally, I raise the possibly that using the LaTRIPP paradigm to model and score sociometric data will result in a *disattenuation* of correlations between preference constructs and other constructs in the nomothetic network. In the data I just described, the correlation between "like most" and "like least" is −0.03 using limited nominations; using optimally scaled unlimited nomination scores, the correlation is −0.26. Clearly, given the restricted range of the forced-nomination procedure, the empirical finding that "like most" scores and "like least" scores are uncorrelated is an artifact of the measurement process; using a theoretically optimal measurement process results in a moderately negative correlation, as one might naturally expect. Our preliminary work in investigating the effects this may have on estimates of stability show that disattenuation results in significantly greater long-term stability (Cillessen, Bukowski, and Haselager, this volume).

What, then, are the implications of the model for sociometric practice? First, the model suggests the basis for empirically establishing the difference between the constructs of friendship and preference. This evidence, if indeed empirically validated, suggests that one should be careful when choosing the nature of the presented stimulus. Second, I have argued elsewhere (Terry, 1999) that under the present circumstances sociometry, as employed here, may be thought of more as a personality test, wherein the traits of likability, unlikability, and popularity are actually being measured rather than social acceptance. Of course, social acceptance will clearly be related to these three personality characteristics, so the distinction may seem to many as over-refined. However, I propose that what we currently define as the aggregate judgment of social acceptance be replaced by the notion of an aggregate judgment of an individual's characterization as being "socially acceptable"; likewise, social rejection should be replaced with "socially unacceptable." This is consistent with the trait concept underlying Kelley's model that such attributions are indicative of dispositional characteristics. "Social acceptance" is defined specific to a group, whereas the notion of "socially acceptable" would likely be more generalizable to other groups.

Third, it is important to recognize that one must simultaneously consider the perceived with the perceiver. Earlier sociometrists such as Moreno (1946), Northway (1946), Criswell (1946), and Bjerstedt (1956) all noted the need to consider the possibility that different perceptual frameworks would be found when making judgments of others; to properly understand the phenomenon is to discover what, if any, common perceptual framework they all share. The model proposed here does exactly that, by recognizing and modeling the different thresholds and sensitivities that individuals have and mathematically relating them to the common latent factor or trait that underlies the entire process. As proposed here, the model is consistent with Kelley's (1967) theory that implies that these judgments are consistent with the attribution of dispositional character traits. This does not mean that such traits are, in fact, dispositional. It simply means that the attributional process underlying sociometric choice is consistent with that interpretation.

Fourth, it may require that we reconsider our understanding of the construct of peer acceptance. As noted by Parker and others (1995), most sociometricians regard the social acceptance construct as conceptually and operationally describing a set of preferences and attitudes of individual members of a peer group that are independent, additive, and interchangeable. In this sense, then, the only thing of any importance in assessing social acceptance is the nature of the judgment (liking-popular) and not the source of the judgment.

The model proposed here suggests modifications of this view. First, preferences are only "locally" independent; that is, individual preferences of members are in fact correlated via their association with the common latent trait; once the trait (likability) is accounted for, then all preferences are, in fact, independent. If the individual member's preferences were not correlated at the global level, then the data would be multidimensional; our data suggest that this is not the case.

Second, the preferences are additive but on a logarithmic scale (see Equation 1). Also, the model indicates that a weighted additive process is needed to sufficiently explain the data. Finally, the source of a nomination does indeed matter. Only by considering the very reasonable proposition that individuals may vary in their sensitivity to social phenomena do we obtain a well-fitting model. This in turn suggests that we must make allowances for who the nominations come from when forming an optimal quantitative representation of the construct.

A number of interesting questions remain if we conditionally accept the model. For instance, we do not know what effects the remeasuring of the foundational constructs of social acceptability and unacceptability will have on the assignment of individuals to social status groups. We do not know whether the use of this method will change our understanding of the relations between social status and behavior. We do not know whether this method may lead to improved methods for collecting sociometric data that are more efficient than our old methods. And we do not know how the model will fare in helping researchers look at the very nature of social interaction in increasingly multicultural, diverse groups. Yet I suspect that because of the richness of the model, such questions may be more profitably investigated within the LaTRIPP paradigm than in the more commonly used methods of sociometry.

A reasonable way to evaluate the importance of a new model is the extent to which it provides a fruitful paradigm for further research. I have suggested here that the model I propose can, in fact, give reason for the field to reevaluate the substantive meaning of sociometric data. It is my hope that new insights will be forthcoming based on this reconceptualization. To the extent that this happens, the model will be a success.

References

Anastasi, A. *Psychological Testing* (6th ed.). New York: Macmillan, 1988.

Anderson, J. C., and Gerbing, D. W. "Some Methods for Respecifying Measurement Models to Obtain Unidimensional Construct Measurement." *Journal of Marketing Research*, 1982, *19*, 453–460.

Anderson, J. C., and Gerbing, D. W. "Structural Equation Modeling in Practice: A Review and Recommended Two-Step Approach." *Psychological Bulletin*, 1988, *103*, 411–423.

Asher, S. R. "Recent Advances in the Study of Peer Rejection." In S. R. Asher and J. D. Coie (eds.), *Peer Rejection in Childhood* (pp. 3–14). New York: Cambridge University Press, 1990.

Asher, S. R., and Dodge, K. A. "Identifying Children Who Are Rejected by Their Peers." *Developmental Psychology*, 1986, *22*, 444–449.

Asher, S. R., and Hymel, S. "Children's Social Competence in Peer Relations: Sociometric and Behavioral Assessment." In J. D. Wine and M. D. Smye (eds.), *Social Competence* (pp. 125–157). New York: Guilford Press, 1981.

Baker, F. B. *Item Response Theory: Parameter Estimation Techniques.* New York: MacMillan, 1992.

Birnbaum, A. "Some Latent Trait Models and Their Use in Inferring an Examinee's Ability." In F. M. Lord and M. R. Novick (eds.), *Statistical Theories of Mental Test Scores* (pp. 397–472). Reading, Mass.: Addison-Wesley, 1968.

Bjerstedt, A. "Sociometric Relations in Elementary School Classes." *Sociometry*, 1955, *18*, 147–152.

Bjerstedt, A. "The Methodology of Preferential Sociometry: Selected Trends and Some Contributions." *Sociometry Monographs*, 1956, *37*, 14–155.

Bock, R. D., and Aitkin, M. "Marginal Maximum Likelihood Estimation of Item Parameters: Application of an EM Algorithm." *Psychometrika*, 1981, *46*, 443–459.

Bogardus, E. S. "Measuring Social Distance." *Journal of Applied Sociology*, 1925, *9*, 299–308.

Bronfenbrenner, U. "The Measurement of Sociometric Status, Structure and Development." *Sociometric Monographs*, 1945, *6*, 1–80.

Bukowski, W. M., and Hoza, B. "Popularity and Friendship: Issues in Theory, Measurement, and Outcome." In T. J. Berndt and G. W. Ladd (eds.), *Peer Relationships in Child Development* (pp. 15–45). New York: Wiley, 1989.

Coie, J. D., and Dodge, K. A. "Continuities and Changes in Children's Social Status: A Five-Year Longitudinal Study." *Merrill-Palmer Quarterly*, 1983, *29*, 261–281.

Coie, J. D., Dodge, K. A., and Coppotelli, H. "Dimensions and Types of Social Status: A Cross-Age Perspective." *Developmental Psychology*, 1982, *18*, 557–570.

Criswell, J. H. "Foundations of Sociometric Measurement." *Sociometry*, 1946, *9*, 7–13.

Cronbach, L. J., and Meehl, P. E. "Construct Validity in Psychological Tests." *Psychological Bulletin*, 1955, *52*, 281–302.

Embretson, S. "Construct Validity: Construct Representation Versus Nomothetic Span." *Psychological Bulletin*, 1983, *93*, 179–197.

Gronlund, N. E. "Generality of Sociometric Status over Criteria in Measurement of Social Acceptability." *Elementary School Journal,* 1955, *56,* 173–176.

Gronlund, N. E. *Sociometry in the Classroom.* New York: Harper, 1959.

Guilford, J. P. *Psychometric Methods* (2nd ed.). New York: McGraw-Hill, 1954.

Hambleton, R. K., and Swaminathan, H. *Item Response Theory: Principles and Applications.* Boston: Kluwer, 1985.

Harmon, L. R. "A Note on Pepinsky's Analysis of 'Validity' and 'Reliability' of Sociometric Data." *Educational and Psychological Measurement,* 1949, *9,* 747–748.

Hattie, J. A. "Methodological Review: Assessing Unidimensionality of Tests and Items." *Applied Psychological Measurement,* 1985, *9,* 139–164.

Holland, P. W., and Leinhardt, S. "The Structural Implications of Measurement Error in Sociometry." *Journal of Mathematical Sociology,* 1973, *3,* 85–111.

Iacobucci, D. "Derivation of Subgroups from Dyadic Interactions." *Psychological Bulletin,* 1990, *107,* 114–132.

Jackson, D. N. "A Model for Inferential Accuracy." *Canadian Psychologist,* 1972, *13,* 185–195.

Kelley, H. H. "Attribution Theory in Social Psychology." In D. Levine (ed.), *Nebraska Symposium on Motivation* (Vol. 15, pp. 192–238). Lincoln: University of Nebraska Press, 1967.

Kindermann, T. "Children's Development Within Peer Groups: Using Composite Social Maps to Identify Peer Networks and to Study Their Influences." In W. M. Bukowski and A.H.N. Cillessen (eds.), *Sociometry Then And Now: Building on Six Decades of Measuring Children's Experiences with the Peer Group* (pp. 55–82). San Francisco: Jossey-Bass, 1998.

Ladd, G. W. "Social Networks of Popular, Average, and Rejected Children in School Settings." *Merrill-Palmer Quarterly,* 1983, *29,* 283–307.

Lord, F. M. *Applications of Item Response Theory to Practical Testing Problems.* Hillsdale, N.J.: Erlbaum, 1980.

Lord, F. M., and Novick, M. R. *Statistical Theories and Mental Test Scores.* Reading, Mass.: Addison-Wesley, 1968.

Michelson, L., and Wood, R. "A Group Assertive Training Program for Elementary School Children." *Child Behavior Therapy,* 1980, *2,* 1–9.

Mislevy, R. J., and Bock, R. D. "PC-BILOG 3: Item Analysis and Test Scoring with Binary Logistic Models" [Computer software]. Mooresville, Ind.: Scientific Software, 1990.

Moreno, J. L. *Who Shall Survive? A New Approach to the Problem of Human Interrelations.* Washington, D.C.: Nervous and Mental Disease Publishing Co., 1934.

Moreno, J. L. "Sociometry and the Cultural Order." *Sociometry,* 1943, *8,* 268–272.

Moreno, J. L. "Sociogram and Sociomatrix." *Sociometry,* 1946, *9,* 348–349.

Moreno, J. L. *Sociometry, Experimental Method and the Science of Society.* Beacon, N.Y.: Beacon House, 1951.

Mouton, J. S., Blake, R. R., and Fruchter, B. "The Reliability of Sociometric Measures." *Sociometry,* 1955, *18,* 7–48.

Newcomb, A. F., and Bukowski, W. M. "Social Impact and Social Preference as Determinants of Children's Peer Group Status." *Developmental Psychology,* 1983, *19,* 856–867.

Northway, M. L. "Personality and Sociometric Status: A Review of the Toronto Studies." *Sociometry,* 1946, *9,* 233–241.

Oden, S., and Asher, S. R. "Coaching Children in Social Skills for Friendship Making." *Child Development,* 1977, *52,* 171–178.

Parad, H. W. *Behavioral Consistency and Change in Children During and After Short-Term Residential Treatment: A Multiple-Perspectives Approach.* Unpublished doctoral dissertation, University of North Carolina, Chapel Hill, 1983.

Parker, J. G., Rubin, K. H., Price, J. M., and DeRosier, M. E. "Peer Relationships, Child Development, and Adjustment: A Developmental Psychopathological Perspective." In

D. Cicchetti and D. Cohen (eds.), *Developmental Psychopathology: Vol. 2. Risk, Disorder, and Adaptation* (pp. 96–161). New York: Wiley, 1995.

Pepinsky, P. N. "The Meaning of 'Validity' and 'Reliability' as Applied to Sociometric Tests." *Educational and Psychological Measurement,* 1949, *9,* 39–49.

Price, J. M., and Ladd, G. W. "Assessment of Children's Friendships: Implications for Social Competence and Social Adjustment." In R. J. Prinz (Ed.), *Advances in Behavioral Assessment of Children and Families* (Vol. 2, pp. 121–150). Greenwich, Conn.: JAI Press, 1986.

Rasch, G. "An Item Analysis That Takes Individual Differences into Account." *British Journal of Mathematical and Statistical Psychology,* 1966, *19,* 49–57.

Scott, J. *Social Network Analysis.* London: Sage, 1991.

Singleton, L. C., and Asher, S. R. "Peer Preferences and Social Interaction Among Third-Grade Children in an Integrated School District." *Journal of Educational Psychology,* 1977, *69,* 330–336.

Terry, R. "LaTRIPP: SAS Macros for Facilitating the Scaling of Social Relations Data" [Computer software]. Norman, Okla.: Terry, 1995.

Terry, R. "A Latent Trait Model of Interpersonal Perception: Implications for Sociometric Assessment." Unpublished manuscript, University of Oklahoma, 1999.

Terry, R., and Coie, J. D. "A Comparison of Methods for Defining Sociometric Status Among Children." *Developmental Psychology,* 1991, *27,* 867–880.

Thissen, D. "MULTILOG: Item Analysis and Scoring with Multiple Category Response Models" (Version 6). Mooresville, Ind.: Scientific Software, 1991.

Thissen, D., and Steinberg, L. "Data Analysis Using Item Response Theory." *Psychological Bulletin,* 1988, *104,* 385–395.

Thissen, D., Steinberg, L., Pyszczynski, T., and Greenberg, J. "An Item Analysis for Personality and Attitude Scales: Item Analysis Using Restricted Factor Analysis." *Applied Psychological Measurement,* 1983, *7,* 211–226.

Thompson, G. G. "Children's Groups." In P. H. Mussen (ed.), *Handbook of Research Methods in Child Development* (pp. 821–853). New York: Wiley, 1960.

Wheaton, B., Muthen, B., Alwin, D., and Summers, G. "Assessing Reliability and Stability in Panel Models." In D. R. Heise (ed.), *Sociological Methodology* (pp. 84–136). San Francisco: Jossey-Bass, 1977.

Williams, G. A., and Asher, S. R. "Peer- and Self-Perceptions of Peer Rejected Children: Issues in Classification and Subtyping." Paper presented at the biennial meeting of the Society for Research in Child Development, Baltimore, Apr. 1987.

Wright, J. C., Giammarino, M., and Parad, H. W. "Social Status in Small Groups: Individual-Group Similarity and the Social 'Misfit.'" *Journal of Personality and Social Psychology,* 1986, *50,* 523–536.

ROBERT TERRY is assistant professor in the Department of Psychology of the University of Oklahoma.

4

Sociometric ratings provide detailed information about a perceiver's sentiments toward group members that is not included in sociometric nominations. Ratings data therefore shed a new light on traditional sociometric classification.

A Ratings-Based Approach to Two-Dimensional Sociometric Status Determination

Gerard H. Maassen, Jos L. van der Linden, F. A. Goossens, J. Bokhorst

Until the early eighties, sociometric status was assessed in a one-dimensional way, employing either nominations or ratings. In the nominations-based procedure, all children from a group (usually a classroom group) are asked to nominate peers with whom they would *most like* to undertake a certain activity (for example, playing) and to nominate peers with whom they would *least like* to undertake that same activity. In the ratings-based method all children in a group are asked to indicate on a rating scale how much they like or dislike every other child in the group. Both procedures aim at a one-dimensional classification of social acceptance of individuals within their peer group.

At an early stage the idea of a more refined determination of sociometric status was mooted (Bronfenbrenner, 1944; Dunnington, 1957). Researchers needed to be able to identify not only the *rejected* students but those who, because of their low social visibility, have few contacts with their peers, namely the *neglected* students (Gronlund and Anderson, 1957). Peery (1979) was the first to suggest a two-dimensional model that makes such a distinction possible. On the basis of his proposals, Coie and Dodge (Coie, Dodge, and Coppotelli, 1982; Coie and Dodge, 1983) and Newcomb and Bukowski (1983) developed new procedures by which a classification into

The authors are indebted to Wies Akkermans, with whom we first began the debate on the dimensionality of sociometric status.

five sociometric status groups (popular, rejected, neglected, controversial, and average) can be derived from the positive nomination totals (or "liked most" score, LM) and the negative nomination totals (or "liked least" score, LL) received by the group members. This classification is considered to be two-dimensional; popular, average, and rejected largely correspond to the first dimension (*social preference*), whereas neglected, average, and controversial correspond to the second dimension (*social impact;* see Figure 4.1). The procedures of Coie and others and of Newcomb and Bukowski differ only in the manner in which the LM and the LL scores are processed and in the statistical criteria for allocating participants to a certain status group. At present, both are considered appropriate methods for determining sociometric status and have been applied in numerous studies (see Newcomb, Bukowski, and Pattee, 1993).

Rating scales continued to be applied in the determination of sociometric status (see, for example, French, 1988, 1990), but their use has declined since the beginning of the eighties. The main reason was apparently that rating scales did not lend themselves readily to a classification in the five categories, which had since become popular. Recently, however, Maassen, Akkermans, and van der Linden (1996) developed a procedure—SSrat, covered by computer program SSRAT (Maassen and Landsheer, 1996)—that enables researchers to employ bipolar ratings for such a classification. The introduction of this method revives the need for a comparison between the nomination and the rating procedure. The main issue of this chapter is to explain that, from certain points of view, the rating method is again preferable.

In the course of our argument we address a number of issues. In the first place, it is evident that certain standard practices have arisen within the framework of the distinctive nomination procedures. For instance, in the standard score method of Coie and others (1982) a cut-off criterion of one standard devi-

Figure 4.1. Location of Sociometric Status Groups on the Social Preference and Social Impact Dimensions

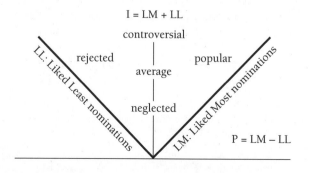

ation is used, and in the probability method of Newcomb and Bukowski (1983) α values are set to .05 or .10. Such practices have not yet been developed with regard to SSRAT.

Before we can reliably compare the nomination and the rating methods, we need further insight into how SSRAT can best be applied. In this chapter we offer some indications. The questions then become the following. First, which method is preferable? Second, if no uniform answer to this question can be given, what are the advantages and disadvantages of the various procedures? Finally, which method can best be used in which situation, considering the observed advantages and disadvantages?

On the basis of these questions, we discuss the function and meaning of sociometry from a measurement perspective. Our particular goal is to offer a solid basis for the identification of children and adolescents who are rejected by their peers. This identification will inform us of the reasons for social rejection and for adequate intervention (Asher and Hymel, 1981; Cillessen and ten Brink, 1991; Cillessen, van IJzendoorn, van Lieshout, and Hartup, 1992). In general, the more one knows about the precision of measurement (reliability and validity) in sociometric procedures, the easier it is to make a well-informed decision about the most appropriate procedure, given the goals and leading questions of the research. Not only can questions of a more fundamental theoretical nature be raised (for instance about the dimensionality of sociometrics) but questions of practical importance can be raised, such as the identification of children who belong to a problem group and should be considered at risk and therefore need specific help (Asher and Coie, 1990).

Are Ratings Still Useful?

Without going into technical detail, there are characteristic differences between the nomination and the rating method that can be explained quickly. On the one hand, using nominations has the distinct advantage of giving respondents an easy task: mentioning only some liked and disliked peers rather than assigning scores to *all* other group members. This makes a nominations-based system more appropriate for large-sized groups or for groups in which not all members know each other. On the other hand, nominations provide only limited information. When using nominations, in principle every respondent has to mention a prescribed number of group members (usually three) as least liked or most liked. (The critical value in the Newcomb and Bukowski procedure is based on such fixed numbers.) However, it is possible, for instance, that the respondent likes all others to some extent, in which case the nomination procedure forces the respondent to be negative about some group members, despite having positive feelings. (In practice, this drawback is mitigated because in most research it is accepted that respondents mention fewer than three nominees.) Although the sympathy or antipathy one feels for the nominated persons is likely to differ, these differences cannot be made explicit with nominations. The same is true of respondents' feelings about group members who are not nominated.

Rating scales, however, enable the researcher to collect information that is more refined and better reflects the respondent's actual feelings about his or her fellow group members. This makes the ratings method particularly apt for moderate-sized groups in which members know each other fairly well (classroom groups for instance). Therefore, in this chapter we restrict ourselves to groups of this type.

We illustrate the aforementioned considerations using data from 172 students collected in eight classrooms in two different settings. The first setting was an elementary school in which 86 children (43 percent girls) from three classrooms participated. The classrooms were a grades two-three combination class ($n = 31$), a grade four-five combination class ($n = 28$), and a grade five-six combination class ($n = 27$). The ages of these children ranged from seven to twelve years. The second setting was a junior high school in which 86 students (50 percent girls) from five seventh-grade classrooms participated (n's per classroom 12, 11, 22, 21, and 20). The ages of these students ranged from twelve to fourteen years.

Two methods of sociometric measurement were used in both settings. All participants were asked to nominate three classmates they liked the most and three classmates they liked the least. Participants were allowed to name fewer peers for both criteria if they were unable to mention three. In addition, participants were asked to rate each classmate on a 7-point bipolar scale ranging from –3 (very nasty) to 3 (very nice). The scale's midpoint (0) reflects a neutral judgment (neither sympathy nor antipathy, just an "ordinary classmate"). Further details about the data collection procedures are presented in Maassen, van der Linden, and Akkermans (1997).

Table 4.1 shows a cross-tabulation of the nominations and the corresponding ratings. The total number of nominations or ratings in each school should equal $\Sigma n_i(n_i - 1)$ summed across the classrooms in that school, where n_i is the number of members of classroom i. The actual totals are somewhat lower because of missing values.

The table allows the following observations. First, the correspondence between positive nominations and ratings was very high. In the two schools, a positive nomination corresponded in 91 percent and 80 percent of the cases, respectively, with a score of 2 or 3 on the rating scale. If students nominated a peer among the three they liked the most, in the vast majority of the cases they also rated this peer highly on the liking scale. In the case of positive nominations, the two methods yielded almost no contradictions: in the two schools combined, a positive nomination corresponded with a rating on the negative end of the rating scale in less than 1 percent of the cases. Second, negative nominations and ratings showed a poorer match. In only 62 percent and 39 percent of the cases, respectively, in which a student was nominated as liked least, the rating was –3 or –2. We noticed that at the

Table 4.1. Correspondence Between Nominations and Ratings in Two Schools: Distribution of Ratings (Relative Frequencies) and Mean Rating Received by Nomination Type

	Ratings							
	−3	−2	−1	0	1	2	3	Mean
Nominations								
Elementary School (n = 86)								
Liked Least	.32	.30	.24	.08	.03	.02	.01	-1.68
(n = 212)								
None	.02	.03	.10	.37	.28	.15	.05	.48
(n = 1840)								
Liked Most	.00	.00	.00	.02	.07	.26	.65	2.53
(n = 242)								
Junior High School (n = 86)								
Liked Least	.22	.17	.28	.22	.08	.02	.00	-1.14
(n = 182)								
None	.03	.03	.07	.28	.31	.19	.08	.63
(n = 837)								
Liked Most	.00	.00	.00	.05	.14	.32	.48	2.18
(n = 203)								

Note: Ratings were made on a 7-point scale.(−3 = dislike very much, 0 = neutral, 3 = like very much.) Data were taken from Maassen, Akkermans, and van der Linden, *International Journal of Behavioral Development*, 1997, *21*, 193. Reprinted with permission of Traylor & Francis Inc.

junior high school level a substantial proportion (22 percent) of the negative nominations were paired with a rating-score indicating indifference (a rating of 0). This is interesting information that the nomination method does not yield.

Although there were fewer matches, the number of contradictions remained low for negative nominations. At the two schools a negative nomination corresponded with a rating at the positive end of the scale in only 6 percent and 10 percent of the cases, respectively. It is not clear whether measurement errors (for example, because the respondents did not understand the assignment) or substantive reasons are involved. Third, when students were not nominated (neither positively nor negatively), their ratings ranged across the complete scale but centered somewhat above the scale's midpoint. Indeed, in a considerable proportion of cases, a person who was not named as "liked most" nevertheless received a favorable liking rating.

We concluded that the restriction of some sociometric methods that students are allowed to nominate only a limited number of peers results in a loss of important information. With nominations, students are able to express the intensity of their affection toward peers only in a limited way. Hence, it is obvious that the admittedly more labor-intensive data collection by means of ratings yields additional information. It becomes important now to find out if and to what extent this additional information is useful for the classification into sociometric status categories.

A Comparison of Nomination and Rating Procedures

The current nomination procedures, the standard score method of Coie and others, and the probability method of Newcomb and Bukowski, have been frequently described elsewhere (see Cillessen, Bukowski, and Haselager, this volume; Cillessen and ten Brink, 1991; Maassen and Landsheer, 1998; Terry, this volume). We need not repeat the exercise here. Similarly, the ratings method SSrat will only be outlined briefly, as this method has been described in detail elsewhere as well. (For a detailed mathematical description and rationale, see Maassen and others, 1996; for a theoretical account, see Maassen and others, 1997.)

We assume that students base their judgments of peers (either with nominations or ratings) on a latent unidimensional bipolar scale of liking. When a student nominates a peer negatively, the latter has been given a position on the negative side of the liking scale; a positively nominated peer has been placed on the positive side. Subsequently, the received positive and negative nominations are processed separately. This concept is also the basis of the rating method, which means that the scores on the positive and negative sides of the bipolar rating scale are processed separately. Following the Peery (1979) model, the following scores are determined for each student: sympathy S (the sum of the positive ratings received), antipathy A (the sum of the absolute value of the negative ratings received), social preference P (S minus A), and social impact I (S plus A). For each rater, the probabilities of giving positive and negative ratings are estimated based on their observed frequencies. We assume as a null hypothesis that a rater uses these probabilities equally for all ratees. We are then able to determine the probability distributions, expected values, and probabilities of the received scores for S, A, P, and I for each ratee (see Maassen and others, 1996, for the mathematical details of the estimation procedure). Finally, criteria are chosen on the basis of significance of these total scores (being smaller than a previously chosen α value) and on a comparison with their expected value under the null hypothesis. Application of these criteria yields a classification of the assessed students into one of the five sociometric status categories.

An essential characteristic of the probability method SSrat is that the ratings are weighted differently depending on the response parameters of the rater. In our view, this is appropriate for the assessment of sociometric status because the scores attributed by a respondent emerge from his or her individual judgment scale. For example, a high rating (for example, 3) received from a student who gives high ratings to all peers carries a different weight than the same rating received from a student who uses high ratings only infrequently. Specifically, a rating of 3 received from a rater who rates all peers as 3 has zero discriminatory value in determining the probabilities of a given ratee's sociometric scores.

An example shown in Table 4.2 illustrates the performance of the nomination and ratings methods. The example contains hypothetical data for a group of eleven individuals. Each member of the group was rated by the ten others on a 7-point bipolar rating scale. The scale's midpoint (in this case 4) stands for a neutral judgment. All higher values correspond to a positive judgment, and all lower values to a negative judgment. The data are arranged in a matrix with rows referring to raters and columns to ratees.

The data in this example were constructed so that there are one or two representatives of each sociometric status category. Person 1 and, to a lesser degree, Person 2 are popular; Persons 3, 8, and (somewhat less) 4 are controversial; and Person 7 is rejected, as is Person 5 (though not to the same degree). At face value, Persons 6 and 10 could be labeled average, whereas Person 11, for whom nobody seems to have any strong feelings, should be regarded neglected. For the remaining group member (Person 9) the qualification is less evident. The scores in Table 4.2 were also constructed so that all group members gave three ratings at the highest level (7) and three ratings at the lowest level (1). If the group members were asked to nominate three "like most" and three "like least" persons we could, discounting errors of measurement, reasonably predict which members would be nominated

Table 4.2. Hypothetical Matrix of Liking Ratings in an Eleven-Person Group and Recoding of Ratings as Nominations

Person	Ratings[a]	Expected Nominations Based on Ratings[b]	Recoding of Nominations[c]
01	−7172117234	− 1 −1 1 0 −1 −1 1 0 0 0	−3132113222
02	7 −721217144	1 − 1 0 −1 0 −1 1 −1 0 0	3 −321213122
03	76 −72317114	1 0 − 1 0 0 −1 1 −1 −1 0	32 −32213112
04	771 −1417564	1 1 −1 − −1 0 −1 1 0 0 0	331 −1213222
05	7672 −511714	1 0 1 0 − 0 −1 −1 1 −1 0	3232 −211312
06	77172 −11234	1 1 −1 1 0 − −1 −1 0 0 0	33132 −11222
07	767216 −7114	1 0 1 0 −1 0 − 1 −1 −1 0	323212 −3112
08	7717211 −454	1 1 −1 1 0 −1 −1 − 0 0 0	3313211 −222
09	76721711 −64	1 0 1 0 −1 1 −1 −1 − 0 0	32321311 −22
10	771724112 −4	1 1 −1 1 0 0 −1 −1 0 − 0	331322112 −2
11	7672171136−	1 0 1 0 −1 1 −1 −1 0 0 −	3232131122 −

Note: Hypothetical ratings were on a 7-point liking scale (1 = not at all; 7 = very much).

[a]Raters are in rows; ratees are in columns.

[b]−1 = liked least, 0 = no nomination, 1 = liked most.

[c]1 = liked least, 2 = no nomination, 3 = liked most.

(see the middle panel of Table 4.2). This constructed example allows us to compare the results of ratings and fixed nominations.

Before discussing the outcomes of the example we would like to point out a useful feature of SSrat. In the right panel of Table 4.2, the expected nominations were recoded into a 3-point scale (1 = liked least nomination; 2 = no nomination; 3 = liked most nomination). Because SSrat is a generalization of the Newcomb and Bukowski (1983) procedure, this latter procedure can be carried out within the SSrat framework simply by using this coding scheme. Subsequently, computer program SSRAT optionally allows application of the classification criteria set by Newcomb and Bukowski (1983).

The data of the example were analyzed according to various methods: (1) CDCnom, the standard score method of Coie and others (1982; using a cut-off point of one standard deviation); (2) NBnom.050, and (3) NBnom.100, the probability method of Newcomb and Bukowski (1983) with .05α and .10α respectively; (4) SSrat.005, (5) SSrat.010, and (6) SSrat.050, the ratings-based procedure SSrat with α's .005α, .010α, and .050α, respectively. (Previous research has indicated that these values cover a relevant range.) The results of these analyses are presented in Table 4.3.

In each of the six analyses, extremely popular or rejected persons (Persons 1 and 7) were easily recognized. Nor did the methods differ with respect to labeling Persons 4, 6, 9, 10, and 11. The advantage of refined measurement when applying rating scales becomes evident in the case of Persons 2 and 5. CDCnom and SSrat with α = .010 or .050 had no difficulty in detecting the typical controversial persons 3 and 8. The NB method (and also SSrat with α set at the strict criterion of .005), however, did not categorize any students as controversial. The fact that the Newcomb and Bukowski method identifies fewer controversial individuals can be explained as follows. Nominations received by clearly controversial persons (as in this example) are more or less equally divided over liking and disliking. The LM score of these participants is then roughly half the maximum possible LM score. The same holds for the LL score. Generally, in small groups neither the LM nor the LL score of these individuals will reach significance, which is necessary for their classification as controversial in the Newcomb and Bukowski system. NBnom may be more effective in detecting controversials in larger groups.

The results of our proposed method seem to be (in the situation studied) no less valid than those of the current nomination methods. The results of the ratings method SSrat with α equal to at least .010 resemble those of the nomination procedure of Coie and others, but the former method was better able to detect popular and rejected group members. In our example, the method of Newcomb and Bukowski seemed to perform less satisfactorily. Of course, we do not pretend that one hypothetical example can demonstrate all-around superiority of the rating method. The example is merely meant to demonstrate that the ratings method is also capable of yielding valid results in small groups. However, the example illustrates principles that will be confirmed in actual data sets, to which we now turn.

In two studies, we collected peer judgments in the form of nominations as well as bipolar ratings. In both cases, the following methods were applied to obtain sociometric status classifications: (1) SSrat with α = .010, (2) SSrat with .025, (3) SSrat with α = .050, (4) NBnom with α = 0.050, (5) NBnom with α = 0.100, and (6) CDCnom. The range of α values for SSrat has been chosen somewhat differently from the example previously discussed, partly in view of the results of that example.

The first study was based on the data from the eight classrooms that yielded the results of Table 4.1. The upper panel of Table 4.4 shows the sociometric status distributions according to the six methods for the eight classroom groups of this study. The data from all eight classrooms were pooled because the status distributions did not differ substantially between the elementary school classrooms and the junior high school classrooms. In order to compare the results with those of the subsequent tables, the 0 midpoint of the original rating scale was transformed to 4. The second study was

Table 4.3. Assignment of Persons to Sociometric Status Types for the Hypothetical Liking Ratings According to Six Classification Methods

Person	Face Value	LM	LL	CDC-nom[a]	NBnom-.050[b]	NBnom-.010[b]	arr	S	A	SSrat-.005[c]	SSrat-.010[c]	SSrat-.050[c]
01	P	10	0	P	P	P	7.0	30	0	P	P	P
02	P–	5	0	A	A	A	6.5	25	0	P	P	P
03	C	5	5	C	A	A	4.0	15	15	A	C	C
04	C–	5	0	A	A	A	4.5	15	10	A	A	A
05	R–	0	5	A	A	A	1.5	0	25	R	R	R
06	A	2	2	A	A	A	4.0	9	9	A	A	A
07	R	0	10	R	R	R	1.0	0	30	R	R	R
08	C	5	5	C	A	A	4.0	15	15	A	C	C
09	A–	1	3	A	A	A	2.8	4	16	A	A	A
10	A	0	3	A	A	N	3.6	7	11	A	A	A
11	N	0	0	N	N	N	4.0	0	0	N	N	N

Note: LM = liked most, LL= liked least, *arr* = average rating received, S = sympathy, A = antipathy, P = popular, R = rejected, N = neglected, C = controversial, A = average.

[a]CDCnom = nominations, standard score method of Coie, Dodge, and Coppotelli (1982).

[b]NBnom.050 and NBnom.010: nominations, probability model of Newcomb and Bukowski (1983) with α's = .05 and .10, respectively.

[c]SSrat.005, SSrat.010, and SSrat.050: ratings probability model with α's = .005, .010, and .050, respectively.

Table 4.4. Distribution of Sociometric Status Types (Percentages) According to Six Classification Methods in Two Studies

Method	Popular	Rejected	Controversial	Neglected	Average
		Study 1 ($n = 172$)			
Ratings					
SSrat.010	10	13	1	5	70
SSrat.025	19	17	1	6	58
SSrat.050	23	20	1	8	48
Nominations					
NBnom.050	2	11	4	9	74
NBnom.100	9	15	5	13	56
CDCnom	17	16	5	16	47
		Study 2 ($n = 157$)			
Ratings					
SSrat.010	15	17	0	1	67
SSrat.025	23	18	0	2	57
SSrat.050	29	21	0	4	46
Nominations					
NBnom.050	10	11	1	3	75
NBnom.100	15	15	7	10	53
CDCnom	13	13	5	9	60

Note: Study 1: results are a reanalysis of the data from Maassen, Akkermans, and van der Linden, *Small Group Research*, 1996, *27*, 68. Reprinted with permission by Sage Publications Inc. Study 2: results are a reanalysis of the data from Maassen, Goossens, and Bokhorst, *Journal of Social Behavior and Personality*, 1998, *26*, 266. Reprinted with permission from Robert A. C. Stewart.

a new study with 157 children (49 percent girls) from six first- and second-grade classrooms (Maassen, Goossens, and Bokhorst, 1998). The classroom sizes (with the number of participating children between parentheses) in this study were twenty-eight (twenty-three), twenty-seven (twenty-six), thirty-two (twenty-seven), thirty (twenty-nine), twenty-eight (twenty-six), and thirty-one (twenty-six). The ages of the children in Study 2 varied from six years, seven months to eight years, ten months. The lower panel of Table 4.4 shows the sociometric status distributions for this second study.

Table 4.4 shows clear differences between the results of the nomination and the rating procedures. Using an α of .050 or less, SSrat assigned hardly any students to the controversial status group, whereas under these conditions the percentage of neglected children was considerably lower than with CDCnom. This phenomenon deserves comment.

SSrat is certainly able to detect clear cases of neglected or controversial status, as was demonstrated in the previous example. That SSrat repeatedly proves to be more discriminating in identifying persons as neglected or controversial than the traditional methods is readily understood. Being neglected according to SSrat, for instance, means that many peers expressed no particular degree of liking or disliking for the person in question (a neutral rating), whereas a neglected person in the nominations procedure is mentioned by very few peers as either liked most or liked least, which naturally occurs more often. Technically, this implies that a significantly low or high SSrat impact score is rare, whereas the fixed cutting score in CDCnom results in almost fixed-sized categories of neglected or controversial persons (see also Newcomb and Bukowski, 1983).

Other remarkable differences concern the popular and rejected groups. With $\alpha = .050$, SSrat assigns much larger percentages of students to the popular or rejected status groups than the nomination procedures do. Choosing sufficiently low α's reduces the percentages of popular and rejected students in SSrat to below those of NBnom or CDCnom. We now elaborate on the delimitation of the popular and the rejected groups.

By collecting ratings, a validation of the assignments to the popular or rejected groups is in a certain sense possible. We base our view on the following considerations. First, the average rating a student receives from peers (*arr*) is comparable across groups of different sizes. Second, an out-of-range criterion can be derived from *arr*, counting the number of anomalies of a distribution. We consider as anomalies those cases where a student with an *arr* below the neutral scale point (4) is nevertheless classified as popular, and those cases where a student with an *arr* above the neutral scale point is classified as rejected.

Tables 4.5 and 4.6 show the composition of various groups of popular and rejected children according to the nomination methods and SSrat using different α levels. For each of these two status groups, the mean, standard deviation, maximum, and minimum of the liking ratings are given as obtained with each of the six computational methods considered. The variable *arr* and the out-of-range criterion provide an indication of the quality of the various distributions.

Although SSrat with $\alpha = .05$ in both studies produced a considerably larger popular group than the nomination procedures did, its *arr*-characteristics were very favorable: a higher mean and a higher minimum score. Lowering the α level makes the distribution more selective: the size of the popular group decreases while the *arr*-characteristics become more extreme. With an α level of .01, the size of the popular group according to SSrat fell within the range of the group sizes produced by CDCnom or NBnom.

A similar pattern of findings emerged for the rejected group. In both studies, SSrat with $\alpha = .05$ assigned considerably more children to the rejected group than the nomination procedures did, whereas its *arr*-characteristics did not indicate a stricter selection. Lowering the α level to .01 brought the group size of SSrat near the sizes produced by the nomination methods. In Study 1 (see Table 4.5), SSrat then performed comparably with CDCnom or NBnom. In Study 2 (see Table 4.6), SSrat with $\alpha = .01$ was the preferred procedure. The *arr* showed a lower mean and a lower maximum score and no longer

Table 4.5. Descriptive Statistics of the Average Ratings Received by Popular and Rejected Children Identified with Six Classification Methods ($n = 172$)

Method	M	SD	Min	Max	n	%	Out of Range[a]
Total	4.07	.73	1.84	5.54	172	100	
Popular							
SSrat.010	4.97	.36	4.40	5.54	18	10	0
SSrat.025	4.82	.41	3.82	5.54	32	19	1
SSrat.050	4.79	.39	3.82	5.54	39	23	1
CDCnom	4.54	.44	3.76	5.37	29	17	3
NBnom.050	4.01	.34	3.80	4.40	3	2	2
NBnom.100	4.54	.50	3.80	5.37	16	9	2
Rejected							
SSrat.010	3.15	.57	1.84	3.93	23	13	0
SSrat.025	3.19	.53	1.84	4.04	29	17	1
SSrat.050	3.26	.53	1.84	4.04	35	20	1
CDCnom	3.16	.60	1.84	4.21	28	16	1
NBnom.050	3.10	.53	1.84	3.85	19	11	0
NBnom.100	3.25	.54	1.84	4.00	26	15	0

Note: Results are a reanalysis of the data from Maassen, Akkermans, and van der Linden, *Small Group Research*, 1996, 27, p. 72. Reprinted by permission of Sage Publications Inc.

[a]For popular: number of popular persons with an average rating received less than 4.0; for rejected: number of rejected persons with an average rating received larger than 4.0.

manifested any anomalies. In the discussion section to follow, we return to the difference in classification results between the ratings- and nominations-based procedures.

Nominations and Ratings in Longitudinal Research

Most research studies that deal with sociometric status aim at detecting students who are rejected by their peers. An important part of this literature is a concern with whether these students remain permanently in the rejected category or whether they succeed in gradually attaining a different sociometric status. To address this issue, we need to pay attention to the performance of sociometric status determination in longitudinal research.

Traditionally, researchers have assumed that ratings are more reliable than nominations (Asher and Hymel, 1981). A concomitant assumption is that more reliable rating scores mean more reliable classifications based on

Table 4.6. Stability Coefficients (Cohen's κ) of Sociometric Status Classifications from Time 1 to Time 2 Using Different Classification Methods

Method	M	SD	Min	Max	n	%	Out of Range
Total	4.48	.76	2.12	6.00	157	100	
Popular							
SSrat.010	5.38	.27	4.96	5.81	24	15	0
SSrat.025	5.29	.27	4.81	5.81	36	23	0
SSrat.050	5.25	.28	4.73	5.81	45	29	0
CDCnom	5.18	.30	4.43	5.81	20	13	0
NBnom.050	5.19	.24	4.85	5.81	15	10	0
NBnom.100	5.15	.28	4.43	5.81	24	15	0
Rejected							
SSrat.010	3.24	.42	2.12	4.08	27	17	1
SSrat.025	3.28	.45	2.12	4.23	29	18	2
SSrat.050	3.35	.47	2.12	4.35	33	21	3
CDCnom	3.36	.53	2.12	4.39	21	13	1
NBnom.050	3.37	.67	2.12	5.12	18	11	2
NBnom.100	3.48	.71	2.12	5.12	23	15	4

Note: Data were taken from Maassen, Goossens, and Bokhorst, *Journal of Social Behavior and Personality*, 1998, 26, 268. Reprinted with permission from Robert A. C. Stewart.

ratings. This argument is of great importance to longitudinal research. Conclusions about the stability or change of students' sociometric classifications must be based on the most reliable classification systems. With the introduction of SSrat it has become possible for the first time to compare the reliability of a two-dimensional classification system based on ratings with the reliability of a classification system based on nominations. Unfortunately, we have so far at our disposal only longitudinal data that consist of sociometric status determinations separated by yearly intervals. With yearly intervals, we can hardly speak of reliability in test-retest form. We therefore prefer to discuss this issue in terms of "stability" rather than "reliability," where stability means replicability of measurements within a reasonable period. High stability is, of course, not the main aim in a longitudinal determination of sociometric status. Nevertheless, the differential stability of findings produced by different techniques is an indication of the relative utility of these techniques. If ratings are indeed more reliable than nominations, then sociometric status determined by ratings will be more stable than when nominations are used. This expectation is supported by the fact that SSrat uses refined information, as was shown earlier.

In this context, the study by Maassen and others (1998; referred to earlier as Study 2) produced notable results. The design of this study was not completely longitudinal in the sense that ratings as well as nominations had been collected at several points in time. In May 1996, students provided nominations as well as 7-point ratings; one year earlier, when SSrat was not yet available, the same students had provided nominations only. It is therefore possible to determine stabilities for the nomination method over a one-year time interval. Furthermore, stabilities across methods can be calculated, that is, for a first measurement by means of nominations and a second measurement by means of ratings. The results of these comparisons are presented in Table 4.7.

The stability of the CDCnom and NBnom (with $\alpha = .10$) classifications, expressed in Cohen's κ, was strikingly low. Even more striking is the fact that these statistics are noticeably lower than the cross-method stabilities with SSrat using different α values. The stability of NBnom with $\alpha = .05$ was slightly higher than the stabilities of CDCnom and NBnom with $\alpha = .100$, but still not higher than the cross-method stabilities of the nomination with the ratings methods. In our view, this can be explained by assuming that the classifications based on ratings are less influenced by the unreliability of measurement.

A more definitive impression of the stability of the ratings method could be obtained if nominations as well as ratings were elicited from the respondents at successive measurement times. In addition, attempts should be made to ensure that the validation is performed by means of substantive variables. We recently collected such data, and a first general analysis shows that the stability of the different variants of the rating method is considerably higher than that of the nomination method, as expected. Cohen's κ ranged from .44 to .51 for the different SSrat variants but ranged from .28 and .30 for the nomination variants. When the rejected group is the focus

Table 4.7. Stability Coefficients (Cohen's) κ of Sociometric Status Classifications from Time 1 to Time 2 Using Different Classification Methods

Classification Method at Time 2 (1996)	Classification Method at Time 1 (1995)		
	CDCnom	NBnom.050	NBnom.100
CDCnom	.15	–	–
NBnom.050	.22	–	–
NBnom.100	.16	–	–
SSrat.010	.21	.24	.23
SSrat.025	.20	.24	.26
SSrat.050	.20	.23	.26

Note: These results are a reanalysis of the data from the Maassen, Goossens, and Bokhorst, *Journal of Social Behavior and Personality*, 1998, 26, 269. Reprinted with permission of Robert A. C. Stewart.

of interest, the classification results seem to favor SSrat with a low α value (for example .01). Analysis of these data will be published in more detail elsewhere.

Summary and Discussion

Sociometric status determination by means of ratings requires greater efforts from the researcher and from the participants in a study than nominations do. We have shown that these extra efforts yield relevant extra information. We would like to point out that in our research and in this chapter we have restricted ourselves to bipolar 7-point rating scales. In our view, the 7-point scale does justice to the character of the rating scale (collection of refined information). A rating scale with more response categories would probably not give more precise measurement because the added difficulty of the respondents' task would be limiting. Strictly speaking, this means of course that the conclusions drawn in this chapter apply only to rating scales with seven scale points.

SSrat enables the researcher to derive from peer ratings a classification into the five sociometric status categories that are by now established in child and adolescent research. Studies in which sociometric status was determined by means of nominations have shown that the resulting classifications can manifest striking differences. Because additional information is collected by ratings, and because ratings data can be processed in a more refined way, we have more confidence in the usefulness of this procedure.

A question that remains is which α value for SSrat should be preferred. Generally, at $\alpha = .05$, SSrat yields fewer neglected and controversial persons than the nomination procedures.[1] Various perspectives offer insight into the question of the best method to identify controversial and neglected persons. Controversial persons experience both sympathy and antipathy from relatively many group members. As indicated by Bukowski and Newcomb (1985), this is reflected in the standard deviation of the received ratings for controversial students. The average ratings received by members of the controversial group are expected to show the largest standard deviation. Because in our research with ratings only small numbers of individuals were classified as controversial, further research in this direction was not pursued in the current study.

According to the nomination method, neglected persons are persons who are favored by only a few group members and who are rejected by few. This does not warrant an unequivocal conclusion that these individuals are neglected. For all kinds of reasons they may be unknown to others, or they may not be the others' favorite but possibly "second best" or "second worst." According to the ratings method, "neglected" persons evoke feelings of neither sympathy nor antipathy with many group members. This can also apply to persons who are unknown in their group, but the scores in the rating procedure can express being "second best or second worst." Thus, the "neglected" category seems to be better determined in a rating procedure.

Validation studies looking at the connection between the classification along the social impact dimension and other variables intended to measure social impact will, of course, provide the deepest insight. We have recently begun such studies (which will be reported in detail elsewhere). We found that SSrat with $\alpha = .05$ yields smaller groups of neglected and controversial persons which did, however, meet an anticipated pattern of average scores on the substantive validation variables, unlike the groups identified by limited nominations.

We also ascertained that SSrat with $\alpha = .05$ generally yields more popular and rejected persons than nomination procedures do. We recommend using a lower α value (for example, .01) when these status categories are important to the research.[2] There are several indications that this also results in greater precision of classification along the "social preference" dimension than with nominations. Because the "rejected" category plays a central role in most research, we consider this an important advantage of the ratings procedure. The increased reliability of the classification is particularly an advantage in the longitudinal determination of sociometric status. A reliable determination at several points in time is of great importance if firm conclusions are to be drawn about changes of status (in particular from or toward the rejected category, see also Cillessen and others, this volume).

In general, the researcher who applies SSrat with $\alpha = .05$ can expect that the outcomes will not be inferior to those of nomination procedures. Relating our findings about the neglected and controversial groups on the one hand with those concerning the popular and the rejected groups on the other hand allows us to recommend the following. Where the neglected and rejected categories are important to the research, an α value not lower than .05 should be used; when the categories popular or rejected are central to the research, an α of .01 is adequate. A combination of both variants may be used if all five sociometric status categories are important.

The recommendation to use different α values depending on the dimension of peer status one is interested in (social preference P, or social impact I) might seem to argue against the ratings method. However, this is only an apparent disadvantage. It should be kept in mind that according to the Coie and others' (1982) method, $P = z - \mathrm{LM}\, z$ and $I = z_{LM} + z_{LL}$, which are subsequently standardized into z_P and z_I. In groups with considerable consensus about the judgment of the group members the variance of I is small, but it will be inflated by standardization. Our analyses corroborated the point made previously by Newcomb and Bukowski (1983) that application of the cut-off criterion of one standard deviation will cause almost fixed-sized proportions of group members to be assigned to the neglected and controversial categories. A substantive test concerning the classification along the social impact dimension could show that the sizes of these categories are in fact smaller and that it is preferable to use a more severe cut-off criterion along this dimension. However, as far as we know, the results of such a test have not yet been published.[3]

In addition to the diagnostic advantages just discussed, the rating procedure is preferable from other points of view as well. First, this method yields data that are more appropriate for more advanced statistical analyses. Matrices filled with preference data initially form the raw data of the rating procedure. These can be used, for instance, for multidimensional scaling techniques and social network analysis. Second, the ratings method yields variables (*arr* or the average received rating) that are more refined and have a better claim to continuity than similar variables obtained by nomination methods (for example, the total numbers of received positive or negative nominations). This makes the variables produced by the ratings procedure more suitable for follow-up analyses such as simple between-group comparisons or a comparison of results within a group at several points in time and for more refined techniques like multiple regression analysis.

Given its characteristics, the rating procedure has the potential to contribute significantly to two important developments in the application of sociometric methods with children and adolescents. First, it adds specific elements to the methodological scrutiny of the possibilities and limitations of sociometric techniques. Second, it may play an important role in identifying problem groups as a first step toward intervention. The ratings procedure may become an important sociometric tool available in studies where such at-risk groups are followed longitudinally.

Notes

1. Raising the α value, as is often done in the nomination procedure of Newcomb and Bukowski (see also Note 3), is not always useful because the number of neglected and controversial persons in this procedure also depends on a comparison of the observed A and S scores with their expected values.

2. It should be noted that the "validation" carried out is based on the variable *arr*. As far as content is concerned, this is an obvious variable to use. However, both the sociometric status according to SSrat and *arr* are calculated from the same ratings, so that it is not an independent validation in a strict sense. In order to compensate for a possible capitalization on chance, a stricter selection of popular and rejected persons is advisable.

3. The nomination method of Newcomb and Bukowski with $\alpha = .05$ usually qualifies strikingly smaller numbers of children as neglected and controversial than does the method of Coie and others (see also Table 4.4). For some researchers this was a reason to use $\alpha = .10$ rather than .05 (Newcomb and Bukowski, 1984; Terry and Coie, 1991).

References

Asher, S. R., and Coie, J. D. *Peer Rejection in Childhood.* New York: Cambridge University Press, 1990.

Asher, S. R., and Hymel, S. "Children's Social Competence in Peer Relations: Sociometric and Behavioral Assessment." In J. D. Wine and M. D. Smye (eds.), *Social Competence* (pp. 125–157). New York: Guilford Press, 1981.

Bronfenbrenner, U. "A Constant Frame of Reference for Sociometric Research." *Sociometry,* 1944, 7, 40–75.

Bukowski, W. M., and Newcomb, A. F. "Variability in Peer Group Perceptions: Support for the 'Controversial' Sociometric Classification Group." *Developmental Psychology*, 1985, *21*, 1032–1038.

Cillessen, A.H.N., and ten Brink, P.W.M. "Vaststelling van Relaties met Leeftijdgenoten" ["Assessment of Children's Peer Relationships"]. *Pedagogische Studiĭn*, 1991, *68*, 1–14.

Cillessen, A.H.N., van IJzendoorn, H. W., van Lieshout, C.F.M., and Hartup, W. W. "Heterogeneity Among Peer-Rejected Boys: Subtypes and Stabilities." *Child Development*, 1992, *63*, 893–905.

Coie, J. D., and Dodge, K. A. "Continuities and Changes in Children's Social Status: A Five-Year Longitudinal Study." *Merrill-Palmer Quarterly*, 1983, *29*, 261–282.

Coie, J. D., Dodge, K. A., and Coppotelli, H. "Dimensions and Types of Social Status: A Cross-Age Perspective." *Developmental Psychology*, 1982, *18*, 557–570.

Dunnington, M. J. "Investigation of Areas of Disagreement in Sociometric Measurement of Preschool Children." *Child Development*, 1957, *218*, 93–102.

French, D. C. "Heterogeneity of Peer-Rejected Boys: Aggressive and Nonaggressive Subtypes." *Child Development*, 1988, *59*, 976–985.

French, D. C. "Heterogeneity of Peer-Rejected Girls." *Child Development*, 1990, *61*, 2028–2031.

Gronlund, N. E., and Anderson, L. "Personality Characteristics of Socially Accepted, Socially Neglected, and Socially Rejected Junior High School Pupils." *Educational Administration and Supervision*, 1957, *43*, 329–338.

Maassen, G. H., Akkermans, W., and van der Linden, J. L. "Two-Dimensional Sociometric Status Determination with Rating Scales." *Small Group Research*, 1996, *27*, 56–78.

Maassen, G. H., Goossens, F. A., and Bokhorst, J. "Ratings as a Validation of Sociometric Status Determined by Nominations in Longitudinal Research." *Journal of Social Behavior and Personality*, 1998, *26*, 259–274.

Maassen, G. H., and Landsheer, J. A. "SSRAT 2.0: A Program for Two-Dimensional Sociometric Status Determination with Rating Scales" [Computer software]. Utrecht, The Netherlands: Maasen and Landsheer, 1996.

Maassen, G. H., and Landsheer, J. A. "SSRAT: The Processing of Rating Scales for the Determination of Two-Dimensional Sociometric Status." *Behavioral Research Methods, Instruments, and Computers*, 1998, *30*, 674–679.

Maassen, G. H., van der Linden, J. L., and Akkermans, W. "Nominations, Ratings, and the Dimensions of Sociometric Status." *International Journal of Behavioral Development*, 1997, *21*, 179–199.

Newcomb, A. F., and Bukowski, W. M. "Social Impact and Social Preference as Determinants of Children's Peer Group Status." *Developmental Psychology*, 1983, *19*, 856–867.

Newcomb, A. F., and Bukowski, W. M. "A Longitudinal Study of the Utility of Social Preference and Social Impact Sociometric Classification Schemes." *Child Development*, 1984, *55*, 1434–1447.

Newcomb, A. F., Bukowski, W. M., and Pattee, L. "Children's Peer Relations: A Meta-Analytic Review of Popular, Rejected, Neglected, Controversial, and Average Sociometric Status." *Psychological Bulletin*, 1993, *113*, 99–128.

Peery, J. "Popular, Amiable, Isolated, Rejected: A Reconceptualization of Sociometric Status in Preschool Children." *Child Development*, 1979, *50*, 1231–1234.

Terry, R., and Coie, J. D. "A Comparison of Methods for Determining Sociometric Status Among Children." *Developmental Psychology*, 1991, *27*, 867–880.

GERARD H. MAASSEN is associate professor in the Department of Methodology and Statistics of Utrecht University, The Netherlands.

JOS L. VAN DER LINDEN is associate professor in the Department of Educational Sciences of Utrecht University, The Netherlands.

F. A. GOOSSENS is associate professor in the Department of Education of the Free University of Amsterdam, The Netherlands.

J. BOKHORST is a postdoctoral fellow in the Department of Education of the Free University of Amsterdam, The Netherlands.

5

Sociometric status categories are moderately stable in normative samples. However, stable category membership at the level of the individual child both reflects earlier developmental processes and predicts later adjustment outcomes. Individual as well as group contextual factors explain the stability of sociometric status.

Stability of Sociometric Categories

Antonius H. N. Cillessen, William M. Bukowski, Gerbert J. T. Haselager

The concept of stability plays an important role in the measurement of children's peer relations. This chapter focuses on the temporal stability of children's peer relations, as assessed with sociometric methods. Even before the use of sociometrics, researchers studied the stability of social structure in children's groups. As early as 1926, Beth Wellman observed the stability of children's playmates and workmates across a five-month period (Wellman, 1926, in Glidewell, Kantor, Smith, and Stringer, 1966). In the first sociometric study with school-age children (Moreno, 1934), stability data were already being collected. Moreno asked kindergarten through eighth-grade children to select their preferred classmates and repeated this across seven-week and two-year time intervals. He concluded that the initial social organization of the classroom groups persisted over time, even across two years and in spite of large changes in the composition of the groups. Moreno (1934) also conducted a stability study with fourteen- to eighteen-year-old boys in high school. The boys' peer preferences were obtained two months into the school year and again three months later. The results of this study indicated that 92 percent of the boys' first choices and 82 percent of their second choices remained unchanged across the three-month interval (Moreno, 1934).

Ever since this first work, understanding the stability of sociometric status has remained important throughout the history of the study of peer

The first author was supported by a summer fellowship from the University of Connecticut Research Foundation. Also, the authors wish to thank Jim Green, Julie Hubbard, and Kees van Lieshout for their helpful comments.

relations (see, for example, Bukowski and Hoza, 1989; Bullock, Ironsmith, and Poteat, 1988; Gronlund, 1959; Hartup, 1983; Hymel, 1983; McConnell and Odom, 1986; Williams and Gilmour, 1994; Witryol and Thompson, 1953). Given the importance of the topic, the first goal of this chapter is to review the current evidence for the temporal stability of sociometric status; the second is to discuss recent conceptual developments that shed light on the causes and consequences of stability of sociometric status.

Stability of Sociometric Categories

Before we begin our discussion of the stability of sociometric status, it is important to identify the dimensions this construct comprises and to discuss the means by which these dimensions are measured.

Two-Dimensional Classification Systems. Ever since the earliest days of sociometry, it has been recognized that interpersonal relationships and experiences should be understood according to two fundamental dimensions: (1) the positive or attractive forces that bring persons together and (2) the negative or repulsive forces that keep persons apart. Measures of these positive forces (of how attractive a child is to others) have been referred to by various terms like *acceptance* (Northway, 1946), *choice* (Lemann and Solomon, 1952), and *most liked* (Coie and others, 1982). Measures of the negative forces have been referred to as *rejection* (Coie and others, 1982). These two fundamental dimensions have been combined to form two new superordinate dimensions. One is an index of relative likableness and is defined as the difference between one's acceptance and rejection in the peer group. This index has been referred to as *preference* (Peery, 1979). The second superordinate dimension is an index of a child's visibility in the group. This score, often referred to as *impact,* is the sum of one's acceptance and rejection scores.

Typically, five status groups (popular, rejected, neglected, controversial, and average) are distinguished, based on the orthogonal dimensions of social preference and impact. To obtain this classification, three systems of data collection and quantification have been used most frequently. These were developed by Coie, Dodge, and Coppotelli (1982), Newcomb and Bukowski (1983), and Asher and Dodge (1986), and therefore have been labeled the CDC-system, NB-system, and AD-system, respectively (Terry and Coie, 1991). In the CDC- and NB-systems, data have been collected using positive and negative nominations (fixed or unlimited). The AD-system also uses positive nominations, but lowest "play" ratings instead of negative nominations.

The CDC- and NB-systems differ in their method of quantification (Newcomb and Bukowski, 1984). The CDC-system uses what has been labeled the standard score method. In this method, children are assigned to status groups based on standardized scores for liked most, liked least, social preference, and social impact. Rejected children, for example, have a standard preference score less than -1, standard "liked least" score less than 0, and standard "liked most" score greater than 0. The NB-system uses the probability method, assigning children to status groups based on the probabilities associated with the numbers of nominations received. In this system, rejected children are those who have a higher-than-chance "liked least" score and a "liked most" score at or below the mean. In the AD-system, positive nominations and lowest "play" ratings are entered into the standard score computational model to assign children to status types analogous to the CDC-method.

An important question is whether these three systems are consistent in their assignment of children to status types. Terry and Coie (1991) found an 88 percent overlap in status type membership between the CDC- and NB-systems and concluded that these two systems are virtually identical (after certain methodological adjustments). Asher and Dodge (1986) found 91 percent agreement between the CDC- and AD-systems. Terry and Coie (1991) found lower correspondence between these two systems, but correspondence increased with the age of the participants. Overall, reasonable ground exists to compare the results from studies that have used these systems.

Stability of Two-Dimensional Classification Systems. In studies on the stability of sociometric classifications, children's status types are determined at two points in time (across intervals of various lengths). The resulting data form a correspondence table of Time 1 by Time 2 status. The cells of this matrix contain the frequencies of each combination of types over time. High stability is indicated by high diagonal and low off-diagonal frequencies. Two statistics have been used to summarize this: percent agreement and Cohen's κ. Both have been used for the overall system and for the individual types. Percent agreement overall is the percentage of all children at Time 1 who retained their initial status at Time 2. Percent agreement for a specific type is the percentage of all children of that type at Time 1 who were classified the same at Time 2. Cohen's κ serves the same two functions while correcting for chance agreement resulting from the marginal distributions of the contingency matrix (Cohen, 1960). It is therefore the preferred stability statistic for polychotomous data. Guidelines have been offered to evaluate κ: values larger than .40 indicate moderate stability; values larger than .60 indicate high stability; and values larger than .80 indicate excellent stability (Agresti, 1990; Landis and Koch, 1977).

Given the frequent use of sociometric methods from the 1980s to the present, it is surprising that the stability of status classifications has been addressed in only a dozen studies. The results of these studies are summarized in Table 5.1, organized according to the participants' grade at Time 1 (preschool to high school) and length of the test-retest interval (one to forty-eight months). Interval length has been presented in months to provide an equal comparison basis between the studies. The number of grade transitions involved in each interval is also included in the table (from 0 to 4; a count of 0 means that the test and retest took place within the same school year).

Table 5.1. Summary of Findings of Twelve Studies on the Stability of Sociometric Status Types

Grade at Time 1	Time of Year	Interval to Time 2	Transitions	Study[b]	Stability Percentages[a]						Cohen's κ[a]					
					T	P	R	N	C	A	T	P	R	N	C	A
Preschool	—	+5 m.	0	VM91	39	48	32	54	28	33	.22	.34	.13	.36	.22	.09
Preschool	Fall	+6 m.	0	OB91	—	—	50	—	—	—	—	—	.47	—	—	—
K–Grade 1	Winter	+12 m.	1	PE96	—	—	55	—	—	—	—	—	—	—	—	—
K–Grade 1	Spring	+12 m.	1	CI92	—	58	51	—	—	52	—	.35	.35	—	—	.16
K–Grade 4	Spring	+12 m.	1	GS92	46	14	18	30	10	64	.06	.04	.08	.26	.01	.03
Grade 2 and 4	—	+5 m.	0	AD86	—	49	69	29	18	36	.26	.43	.57	.22	.08	.19
Grade 3	Spring	+12 m.	1	CD83	—	44	47	27	50	—	—	—	—	—	—	—
Grade 3	Spring	+12 m.	1	TC91	—	—	40	—	—	—	.19	.46	.32	.08	.09	.16
Grade 3	Spring	+24 m.	2	TC91	—	—	—	—	—	—	.19	.47	.33	.01	.13	.16
Grade 3 and 5	Spring	+48 m.	4	CD83	23	21	30	24	14	22	.01	-.03	.19	.06	.07	-.15
Grade 4	Fall	+6 m.	0	OL91	—	42	59	28	—	—	—	.36	.54	.18	—	—
Grade 4	Fall	+12 m.	1	OL91	—	42	52	17	—	—	.22	.32	.40	.27	—	—
Grade 4	Fall	+18 m.	1	OL91	—	36	58	11	—	—	.23	.23	.50	.06	—	—
Grade 4	Spring	+12 m.	1	CD83	—	67	29	13	30	—	.17	—	—	—	—	—
Grade 4	Spring	+12 m.	1	TC91	—	—	45	—	—	—	.24	.49	.41	.07	.17	.20
Grade 4 and 5	Spring	+1 m.	0	NB83	61	—	—	—	—	—	.44	.61	.76	.33	.41	.53
Grade 5	Spring	+1 m.	0	NB84	—	65	74	36	41	69	.42	—	—	—	—	—
Grade 5	Spring	+6 m.	1	NB84	—	35	45	18	35	61	.18	—	—	—	—	—
Grade 5	Spring	+12 m.	1	CD83	41	41	48	26	35	—	—	—	—	—	—	—

Table 5.1. Summary of Findings of Twelve Studies on the Stability of Sociometric Status Types (*cont.*)

Grade at Time 1	Time of Year	Interval to Time 2	Transitions	Study[b]	Stability Percentages[a]						Cohen's κ[a]					
					T	P	R	N	C	A	T	P	R	N	C	A
Grade 5	Spring	+12 m.	1	NB84	—	23	24	16	28	73	.15	—	—	—	—	—
Grade 5	Spring	+24 m.	2	NB84	—	34	35	22	28	69	.18	—	—	—	—	—
Grade 6	Fall	+1 m.	0	NB84	—	50	50	39	63	73	.40	—	—	—	—	—
Grade 6	Fall	+6 m.	0	NB84	—	32	35	14	43	75	.23	—	—	—	—	—
Grade 6	Fall	+18 m.	1	NB84	—	18	33	15	31	67	.11	—	—	—	—	—
Grade 6	Spring	+12 m.	1	CD83	—	34	50	29	20	—	—	—	—	—	—	—
Grade 6	Spring	+12 m.	1	NB84	—	27	47	16	37	69	.19	—	—	—	—	—
Grade 7	Spring	+12 m.	1	CD83	—	25	33	10	25	—	—	—	—	—	—	—
Grade 8	Spring	+12 m.	1	CD83	—	50	40	29	14	—	—	—	—	—	—	—
Grade 9–12	Spring	+12 m.	1	FR94	60	35	50	46	24	72	.28	.23	.35	.46	.19	.23

[a]T = total classification system; P = popular; R = rejected; N = neglected; C = controversial; A = average.

[b]Study abbreviations: AD86 = Asher and Dodge (1986); CD83 = Coie and Dodge (1983); CI92 = Cillessen and others (1992); FR94 = Franzoi and others (1994); GS92 = Gresham and Stuart (1992); NB83 = Newcomb and Bukowski (1983); NB84 = Newcomb and Bukowski (1984); OB91 = Olson and Brodfeld (1991); OL91 = Ollendick and others (1991); PE96 = Pettit and others (1996); TC91 = Terry and Coie (1991); VM91 = Vaughn and Mize (1991).

In our review, we distinguished the short-term and the long-term stability of sociometric status. First, studies are reviewed addressing short-term stability. In these studies, the stability of sociometric status was measured across intervals of three months or less (the equivalent of one school semester) and within the context of the same school year (not including a transition from one school year to another). Studies measuring stability over intervals longer than three months or across school year transitions are studies of long-term stability and are discussed separately.

The results shown in Table 5.1 are based on the CDC-system. This was the most commonly used system; data based on this system were available in almost all studies. However, in three studies data based on the CDC-system were not reported, and another system was used. Asher and Dodge (1986) used the AD-system; Ollendick, Greene, Francis, and Baum (1991) used the AD-system; and Cillessen, van IJzendoorn, van Lieshout, and Hartup (1992) used the NB-system. An important question is whether the CDC-, AD-, and NB-systems yield comparable stability findings. Four studies provided answers to this question. The CDC-system yielded lower stabilities for popular and rejected status than the AD-system in a study with preschool children (Vaughn and Mize, 1991). In third and fourth grade, however, the CDC- and AD-systems yielded comparable stabilities (Terry and Coie, 1991), although the NB-system yielded lower estimates than the other two systems in this study. In two studies with fourth through sixth graders (Newcomb and Bukowski, 1983, 1984), the CDC- and NB-systems yielded comparable stabilities across intervals from one month to four years. Based on these studies, it seems acceptable to use the CDC-system as a comparison base at this time. The main caveat is to recognize that its stability estimates may be conservative estimates in samples of young children.

Table 5.1 includes all information that could be located on the stability of two-dimensional systems, with one exception. From the Coie and Dodge (1983) study, only the year-to-year and the four-year stabilities are included. The two- and three-year stabilities were omitted to reduce the total amount of information to be presented. These stabilities were always equivalent to or lower than the one-year stabilities. Four-year stability was included because it is a unique finding and because the authors presented a full stability matrix for which we could compute κ.

An empty cell in Table 5.1 means that the corresponding information could not be obtained from the publication. Percent agreement (uncorrected for chance) was reported more frequently than Cohen's κ . We used the following strategy to maximize the amount of information we could present. If percentages or κ's were not reported, they were computed if a correspondence table was provided or could be reconstructed. One adjustment was made during these computations. Whereas the original CDC-model distinguished an "average" and an "other" group, these were collapsed in a later formulation (Coie and Dodge, 1983). This adjustment was used here as well. If separate stability coefficients were presented for "average" and "other," a new coefficient was computed for the combined average group. This value then was entered in Table 5.1. This adjustment to the average group does not change the original stability values for the extreme status groups.

Short-Term Stability. As indicated in Table 5.1, two studies have addressed the short-term stability of the CDC-system (across three months or less). Newcomb and Bukowski (1983) found 61 percent overall stability and κ values larger than .40 for individual status groups in the spring of fourth and fifth grade. Similarly, Newcomb and Bukowski (1984) found overall κ's around .40 and stability percentages from 36 percent to 74 percent for the status types in the fall of fifth and sixth grade. Thus, acceptable short-term stability has been found for the CDC-system with fourth, fifth, and sixth graders. It should be noted, however, that comparable data are not available for either younger or older age groups.

Long-Term Stability. The remaining data in Table 5.1 address the long-stability of the CDC-system. Overall stability percentages were reported in four studies. Vaughn and Mize (1991) found that 39 percent of preschoolers were classified identically across five months in the same school year. Gresham and Stuart (1992) found the same status type across one year for 46 percent of kindergarten through fourth-grade children. Coie and Dodge (1983) reported that 23 percent of third and fifth graders obtained their initial status again after four years. Finally, Franzoi, Davis, and Vasquez-Suson (1994) found that 60 percent of high school students retained their status from one year to the next.

Overall κ's were reported in a larger number of cases. Two κ's were extremely low. Gresham and Stuart (1992) reported a value of .06, but its meaning is difficult to determine, given the mixed-age composition of their sample. The .01 value found for the Coie and Dodge (1983) data reflects the exceptional time span on which this was based (four years). If these two values are excluded, the remaining κ's fall within a fairly narrow range (.11 to .28, median .19). This suggests that the overall κ's center around .20, with little variation due to age or interval length. Note, however, that none of the overall κ's reached the .40 cut-off for moderate stability.

For each status group separately, the long-term stability results (across more than three months) were as follows (Table 5.1). For the popular group, stability percentages have ranged from 14–67 percent (median 35 percent); κ exceeded .40 in four of the twelve cases where it was reported. Stability for the rejected group ranged from 18–69 percent (median 45 percent); κ reached .40 in six of the thirteen cases. For the neglected group, stability has varied from 10–54 percent (median 23 percent). One of the eleven κ exceeded .40. For "controversial" status, percentages have ranged from 10–50 percent (median 28 percent); none of the eight κ's exceeded the criterion. Finally, stability for the average group has varied from 22–75 percent (median 65 percent), but none of the nine κ's reported exceeded the .40 cut-off, indicating moderate stability.

Based on median percentages, the status groups are ordered as follows from high to low stability: average (65 percent), rejected (45 percent), popular (35 percent), controversial (28 percent), and neglected (23 percent). Of the fifty-three κ's for individual status groups, only eleven (21 percent) were of moderate size; ten of these eleven were for the rejected or popular groups. Thus, while κ's were low in general, they suggested that the rejected and popular classifications are more stable than the remaining three groups.

Age and Interval Length. Comparisons within studies have indicated that the stability of peer status increases with children's age and decreases with the length of the test-retest interval (see, for example, Asher and Hymel, 1981). A comparison across the studies in Table 5.1 provides further insight into this issue. For each finding in Table 5.1, age at Time 1 was determined from the study's method section or estimated using grade and time of year at assessment. Ages subsequently were rounded off at the next half year (range 4.5–16.5 years). As before, number of transitions again correlated highly with interval length and therefore was not considered separately in this analysis.

Using the study results in Table 5.1 as the units of analysis, correlations were computed between children's age, interval length, and the stability statistics. Table 5.2 presents these correlations. (Overall percent agreement is excluded because only four data points were available; see Table 5.1.) These correlations are based on a small number of cases (between nine and twenty-one) and must be interpreted accordingly. However, some interesting findings emerged. First, interval length correlated negatively (–.72) with the κ's for the stability of all sociometric status groups combined. That is, children are less likely to maintain their initial status type over longer time intervals. Second, interval length correlated negatively with the κ's for the

Table 5.2. Correlations of Age at Time 1 and Interval Length with Stability Coefficients for the Overall Classification System and for Separate Sociometric Status Groups

| | Correlations of Age at Time 1 | | Correlations with Interval Length | |
	With Stability Percentages	With Cohen's κ's	With Stability Percentages	With Cohen's κ's
Overall	—	.26	—	–.72*
Popular	–.18	–.01	–.46*	–.62*
Rejected	.01	.27	–.39*	–.44
Neglected	–.18	.24	–.27	–.55
Controversial	.06	.22	–.45	–.46
Average	.61*	.31	–.45	–.73*

stability of popular status (–.62) and average status (–.73) and with the stability percentages of popular status (–.46) and rejected status (–.39). Thus, the stability of popular, average, and rejected status decreased when longer test-retest intervals were considered. Third, age at Time 1 correlated positively with the stability percentage of average status (.61); that is, average status was more stable in samples of older children. We had expected significant correlations between age and the stability of other status types as well, based on the idea that children's peer relations are becoming more stable with age. The absence of these correlations may reflect the less then perfect nature of this exploratory analysis.

Regressing the stability statistics on both variables tested the combined effect of age and interval length as predictors of stability. When combined they explained significant portions of the stability percentage and κ of popular status (16 percent and 27 percent, respectively), the percentage and κ of average status (51 percent and 58 percent), and the overall κ (53 percent). The last finding was the strongest and most interesting: age and interval length significantly predicted the overall κ, $F(2,17) = 11.78$, $p < .001$. As for status dimensions, this analysis indicated that the stability of status types also increased with the age of the participating children and decreased with the length of the test-retest interval. At the level of individual categories, this was found for popular and average status.

Conclusion. The stability of sociometric status types has been studied relatively infrequently. Information about the stability of status types is not available for certain age groups and transitions. This is somewhat surprising, given the pervasive use of status types in the literature. Stability percentages have been moderate; κ's have reached the criterion for moderate stability relatively infrequently. The data suggest that popular and rejected are the most stable status groups. The lower κ's for average than for popular and rejected may reflect the higher base rate of average status, which leads to a larger correction for chance than for the popular and rejected groups.

Future analyses of stability would benefit greatly from the presentation of complete information in the methods or results sections of published reports. In the currently available publications, important information cannot always be recovered. Some studies have included percentages of agreement, but no κ's. Others have provided overall κ's but not for each status type. One solution is to include a concise contingency table so that all statistics can be reconstructed. Studies with mixed-cohort samples frequently have not presented data by cohort, preventing the evaluation of stability across age. It has been difficult in several cases to recover simple information about testing times and interval lengths. It would also be extremely informative to know the stability of the voter population from one testing time to the next. We recommend that these various pieces of information be included in future stability studies. They will enable a further comparison of findings and further insight in the stability of sociometric status types.

Beyond Recording Stability

Recently, researchers have begun to address issues that surpass the mere recording of stability. Four issues are identified and discussed here. First, theoretical perspectives are discussed that address the reasons for the stability of status. Second, researchers are addressing whether the stability of status, in particular rejected status, predicts certain outcomes. A third and related issue is whether stable status is an outcome predicted by earlier child characteristics. Fourth and finally, the issue of stability leads to the question of change. Several studies have been conducted on the responsiveness of sociometric measures to intervention efforts aimed at improving children's peer relations.

Explanations for Stability of Sociometric Status

Sociometric status reflects the relative position of the individual child in the group in which it is being assessed (Coie and Cillessen, 1993). It depends on both the individual (for example, the child's aggressiveness) and the group (for example, the group's norms for aggression, see, Boivin, Dodge, and Coie, 1995; Wright, Giammarino, and Parad, 1986). Both perspectives also need to be considered in explaining the stability of status. Four such explanations can be identified that either take the perspective of the child by focusing on individual behaviors, skills, and experiences as determinants of stability, or the perspective of the group by focusing on the social perceptions and group interactions that contribute to the maintenance of status.

First, the stability of peer status may simply result from the stability of underlying child characteristics. Behavioral, social-cognitive, and emotional characteristics of the individual child are correlated with sociometric status (Crick and Dodge, 1994; Hubbard and Coie; 1994; Newcomb, Bukowski, and Pattee, 1993). If these individual characteristics are stable, sociometric status may be stable as a result. For example, consistent aggression could explain stable "rejection," and consistent prosocial behavior could explain stable "popular" status. This explanation thus reflects an incidental view of the role of peers in development, conceptualizing peer status as a marker variable for underlying competencies or disturbances (Parker and Asher, 1987).

A second explanation focuses on the social experiences of children who differ in peer status. Popular children who frequently interact with others receive regular feedback on the effectiveness of their behavior and may improve their skills accordingly. Rejected children who lack positive peer interactions do not benefit from similar experiences. Status groups are also differentiated in their experiences of friendship (for example, Hartup, 1996) and loneliness (for example, Renshaw and Brown, 1993). In this view, children's social experiences associated with their peer status determine the continuation of their status, consistent with a causal view of the role of peers (Parker and Asher, 1987).

A third explanation for the stability of a peer status concerns the social perception processes taking place in the peer group. An assumption of the previous explanations is that children's social judgments primarily reflect peers' actual behaviors and skills. However, research with adults has shown that social judgments are also based on previous impressions of others, independent of their actual characteristics (for example, Rosenthal, 1994). These previous impressions tend to be resistant to change. Adults, for example, selectively process interpersonal information according to their initial expectations. They also approach others based on their expectations, thereby eliciting responses that confirm their expectations (Snyder, 1984). Evidence exists for the occurrence of similar processes among children (DeLawyer and Foster, 1986; Harris, Milich, Johnston, and Hoover, 1990; Musser and Graziano, 1991; Olson, 1992). For example, children selectively interpret a peer's behavior depending on its valence and their liking for the child (Cirino and Beck, 1991; Hymel, 1986; Rogosch and Newcomb, 1989). Peers also attribute greater hostile intent to a known aggressive peer than a nonaggressive one (Dodge, 1980). These attributions in turn initiate a behavioral cycle in which a peer's earlier displays of aggression are correlated with the subsequent receipt of aggression from others (Dodge and Frame, 1982). These various ways in which peers maintain their social evaluations contribute to the stability of a child's peer group status. Cillessen and Ferguson (1995) found that peers' negative expectations of rejected children are related to the stability of these children's rejected status from one school year to the next.

A fourth and final explanation focuses on the contribution of the child's social self-perceptions. Adults use various strategies to maintain consistency in their self-conceptions (Swann, 1987). For example, adults use behavioral strategies that confirm their self-perceptions, and they selectively interact with others who see them in the same way they see themselves (Swann, 1983). Children may contribute to the maintenance of their own status in similar ways. For example, rejected children often interpret a peer's behavior as motivated by hostile intentions, which mediates the child's own subsequent negative behavior (Coie, 1990). Not many data exist on the impact of social self-perceptions on children's interactions with peers. Rabiner and Coie (1989) found that when children think others will like them, they behave more appropriately in subsequent interactions with new acquaintances and are actually better liked. Further research along these lines is necessary because these strategies of self-verification (Swann, 1983) may contribute in an important way to the stability of children's social standing with peers.

In summary, the stability of peer status may be determined by a complex interplay of individual and group factors that are expected to operate in parallel. Not much is known, however, about their relative importance and how this may change across development. For example, social-perceptual factors may become more important as children's social-cognitive skills mature. In addition, contextual factors need to be considered (Coie, 1990). When children move to new groups (for example, during school transitions), individual behaviors and self-perceptions determine the continuation of previous status. In constant social groups (for example, within the context of one school year), social experiences with peers and peers' perceptions of the child are more important. Understanding factors that maintain peer status is important to determine focal points of intervention for children who are locked in stable patterns of unfavorable peer relations.

Stability as a Predictor Variable

Researchers have examined whether the stability of sociometric status predicts children's concurrent behavior. Cillessen, van IJzendoorn, and Ferguson (1991) identified boys who were stable or unstable popular and stable or unstable rejected across two years in early elementary school. Stable popular boys were more cooperative, resilient, self-confident, and competent than unstable popular boys. Stable rejected boys were more aggressive, disruptive, and impulsive than unstable rejected boys. Vitaro, Gagnon, and Tremblay (1990) followed rejected children from kindergarten to Grade 1 and compared those who remained rejected with those who did not. Stable rejected children were more extreme cases of rejection and were less prosocial in kindergarten than unstable rejected children. In Grade 1, stable rejected children displayed more problematic behaviors than their unstable counterparts. These researchers also found that the externalizing behaviors of stable rejected children increased significantly over time. Pettit, Clawson, Dodge, and Bates (1996) also found that children who were chronically rejected in kindergarten and first grade were more aggressive and less socially skilled than children who were rejected in one year only.

Researchers have also examined whether the stability of status predicts later behavior. Because status measured at one point in time predicts later adjustment (see Parker and Asher, 1987; Coie, Lochman, Terry, and Hyman, 1992), stable status across multiple time points should strongly predict later adjustment. In particular, stable rejected children are expected to be more at risk than any other group for later social adjustment difficulties. Cillessen, Haselager, and van Lieshout (1992) found that the stability of boys' rejection at the beginning of elementary school predicted bullying, low prosocial behavior, withdrawal, victimization, loneliness, and depressive symptoms at the end of elementary school. DeRosier, Kupersmidt, and Patterson (1994) found that stable rejection across three years in middle childhood predicted externalizing, internalizing, and school adjustment problems in the following school year, especially for boys.

Clearly, consistent rejection predicts negative outcomes. It is tempting to conclude that certain social experiences associated with chronic rejection are the causes of these outcomes. This conclusion, however, is warranted only when the extremity of the initial status is controlled for. The heightened risk of stable rejected children may be the result of their more extreme peer experiences (a causal interpretation). However, the more extreme adjustment scores of stable rejected children may also reflect that they were more extreme cases of rejection initially (an incidental interpretation). Sorting out these causal and incidental interpretations in more detail is an important goal for future research.

Stability as an Outcome Variable

An important emphasis in social development research is the prediction of the chronicity of adolescent maladjustment (Coie, Terry, Lenox, Lochman, and Hyman, 1995). Researchers sometimes have used the stability of peer status, in particular stable peer rejection, as a measure of this. In their five-year longitudinal study, Coie and Dodge (1983) found that peer nominations of social behavior in each year enhanced the prediction of status in the following year beyond the prediction made by earlier status. Children who remained popular scored higher on cooperation and leadership and lower on disruption and aggression than other children. Children who remained rejected showed the opposite pattern (low prosocial and high antisocial). Children who remained neglected were particularly shy. Cooperation as well as aggression and disruptive behavior predicted the stability of controversial status. These predictions held from one year to the next, but also across the five-year time span of the study.

Newcomb and Bukowski (1984) used factor scores derived from peer behavioral nominations to predict whether children would remain in a particular status group. They found that school competence and the absence of immature behavior predicted stable popular status. Early aggression and immaturity predicted stability of rejected and controversial status. The investigators could not reliably predict the stability of neglected status.

Vitaro and others (1990) predicted stable rejection in kindergarten and Grade 1 from kindergarten behaviors. Prosocial behavior observed by teachers and sharing observed by peers significantly discriminated stable and unstable rejected boys, but not girls. In a follow-up study including Grade 2, however, Vitaro, Tremblay, Gagnon, and Boivin (1992) found that peer and teacher assessments of antisocial behavior predicted the stability of rejected status for both girls and boys.

These findings are consistent with the general prediction of social status from social behavior. The behaviors that predict membership to a status category also seem to predict stable category membership. Prosocial behavior predicted both incidental and consistent popular status; antisocial behavior predicted both incidental and chronic rejection. These findings suggest that children with the most extreme scores for a social behavior are the most likely to remain in the status group with which the behavior is associated.

Responsiveness to Change

In spite of the various pressures toward stability we have discussed, to what extent can sociometric status be changed? Researchers have been successful in improving peer acceptance or reducing peer rejection through coaching procedures (Ladd, 1981; Oden and Asher, 1977), academic tutoring and social skills training (Coie and Krehbiel, 1984), participation in peer involvement groups in which children interacted with others under a superordinate goal (Bierman and Furman, 1984), and the practice of interactional skills such as conversational skills and positive peer responses (Bierman, 1986).

Not all interventions, however, have yielded similar changes. Mize and Ladd (1990) found changes in the behavior of low-status preschool children as a result of social skills training but not in their level of peer acceptance. Bierman, Miller, and Stabb (1987) were able to influence the behavior of rejected first- through third-grade boys but did not increase their peer acceptance. Gresham and Nagle (1980) effectively used coaching and modeling techniques to improve the social skills of socially isolated third and fourth graders, but only limited effects on sociometric measures emerged. La Greca and Santogrossi (1980) used modeling, coaching, and behavioral rehearsal with poorly accepted third through fifth graders. These children's sociometric scores did not change, even though the intervention led to increased behavior skills, greater knowledge of peer interaction, and more initiation of peer interaction in school. The findings from these studies converged by showing that it is easier to improve children's social behaviors and skills than it is to change their peer acceptance.

Various factors might explain why sociometric measures could be changed in some studies but not in others, such as differences in the children's age or the exact nature of the interventions. It is also important to consider that these interventions have focused primarily on changing individual children's behaviors and skills. As we have indicated, group experiences, social self-perceptions, and perceptions by peers are expected to contribute to the maintenance of social status as well. Bierman and others (1987) suggested that the lack of change of peer rejection in their study may have been the result of negative expectations and stereotypes by peers that are hard to overcome for rejected children. Counteracting these negative group perceptions may be necessary for status improvement. Peer involvement in small collaborative groups with superordinate goals can improve low status, independent of the improvement of individual skills (Bierman and Furman, 1984). Thus, although individual behavior must remain a focus of intervention, peer group factors that contribute to status need to be targeted as well.

Conclusion

Across studies investigating the stability of sociometric status types, about 40 percent of children retained their social status type from one point in time to the next. For the separate status types, roughly 65 percent of average children, 40 percent of popular and rejected children, and 25 percent of controversial and neglected children retained their status type over time. When these stabilities were corrected for chance, the resulting κ statistics indicated moderate stability at best. However, κ is a conservative statistic, and it may be appropriate to compare its values to the κ's for other, similar polychotomous constructs rather than to absolute standards.

The short-term stability of status classifications was acceptable, pointing to satisfactory reliability in those age groups for which this has been considered. It is surprising, though, that this issue has not been addressed more frequently, given the widespread use of sociometric methods. We distinguished the short-term stability of status (across less than three months) from the stability over longer intervals. Typically, the short-term instability of a psychological construct reflects the unreliability of the measure (Allen and Yen, 1979). Instability over longer intervals also reflects changes in the phenomenon under consideration. Pepinsky (1949), however, argued against the application of this distinction to sociometric data. According to Pepinsky, the dynamic nature of social relations causes fluctuations in sociometric data over any period of time. These variations were considered to reflect actual changes in behavior rather than the unreliability of the instrument. Pepinsky went further to argue that high test-retest correlations for sociometric data are not even desirable, as they would indicate that the data do not capture the inherent fluidity of social relations. Although this argument seems extreme, it is consistent with Moreno's emphasis on the dynamical nature of groups.

Sociometric studies differ from one another in more than one aspect of their methodology (for example, quantification method, sociometric criteria, computational models, and nature of the reference groups). An advantage of this heterogeneity of methods is that similar results obtained across studies can be considered robust. A disadvantage is, however, that it is difficult to reach conclusions about the factors influencing stability from a comparison between studies. A few direct comparison studies have been conducted (for example, Hymel, 1983; Terry and Coie, 1991). Many interesting comparisons, however, have not yet been examined systematically. For example, although researchers increasingly are using unlimited nominations (see Terry, this volume), the effect of this on the stability of sociometric data has not yet been investigated. Future research needs to consider the impact of these and other methodological innovations on the stability of sociometric data.

In addition to these methodological points, four conceptual issues were identified that are related to the stability of peer status. Explanations for the stability of sociometric status were discussed, the possibility of change through intervention, and the use of stability as a predictor of outcomes in developmental models of social adjustment. An important goal for future research is to document in more detail the social experiences of children who are consistently rejected but also of those who are consistently popular, and to determine more precisely which experiences and consequences are associated with the stability of sociometric status.

References

Agresti, A. *Categorical Data Analysis.* New York: Wiley, 1990.

Allen, M. J., and Yen, W. M. *Introduction to Measurement Theory.* Monterey, Calif.: Brooks/Cole, 1979.

Asher, S. R., and Dodge, K. A. "Identifying Children Who Are Rejected by Their Peers." *Developmental Psychology,* 1986, *22,* 444–449.

Asher, S. R., and Hymel, S. "Children's Social Competence in Peer Relations: Sociometric and Behavioral Assessment." In J. D. Wine and M. D. Smye (eds.), *Social Competence* (pp. 125–157). New York: Guilford Press, 1981.

Bierman, K. L. "Process of Change During Social Skills Training with Preadolescents and Its Relation to Treatment Outcome." *Child Development,* 1986, *57,* 230–240.

Bierman, K. L., and Furman, W. "The Effects of Social Skills Training and Peer Involvement on the Social Adjustment of Preadolescents." *Child Development,* 1984, *55,* 151–162.

Bierman, K. L., Miller, C. L., and Stabb, S. D. "Improving the Social Behavior and Peer Acceptance of Rejected Boys: Effects of Social Skill Training with Instructions and Prohibitions." *Journal of Consulting and Clinical Psychology,* 1987, *55,* 194–200.

Boivin, M., Dodge, K. A., and Coie, J. D. "Individual-Group Behavioral Similarity and Peer Status in Experimental Playgroups of Boys: The Social Misfit Revisited." *Journal of Personality and Social Psychology,* 1995, *69,* 269–279.

Bukowski, W. M., and Hoza, B. "Popularity and Friendship: Issues in Theory, Measurement, and Outcome." In T. J. Berndt and G. W. Ladd (eds.), *Peer Relationships in Child Development* (pp. 15–45). New York: Wiley, 1989.

Bullock, M. J., Ironsmith, M., and Poteat, M. G. "Sociometric Techniques with Young Children: A Review of Psychometrics and Classification Schemes." *School Psychology Review,* 1988, *17,* 289–303.

Cillessen, A.H.N., and Ferguson, T. J. "Self-Perpetuation Processes in Children's Peer Relations." Unpublished manuscript, University of Connecticut, Storrs, 1995.

Cillessen, A.H.N., Haselager, G.J.T., and van Lieshout, C.F.M. "Children's Problems Caused by Consistent Rejection In Early Elementary School." Paper presented at the Centennial Convention of the American Psychological Association, Washington, D.C., Aug. 1992.

Cillessen, A.H.N., van IJzendoorn, H. W., and Ferguson, T. J. "Social Behavioral and Social Adjustment Differences Between Stable and Unstable Sociometric Groups." Paper presented at the biennial meetings of the International Society for the Study of Behavioral Development, Minneapolis, July 1991.

Cillessen, A.H.N., van IJzendoorn, H. W., van Lieshout, C.F.M., and Hartup, W. W. "Heterogeneity Among Peer-Rejected Boys: Subtypes and Stabilities." *Child Development,* 1992, *63,* 893–905.

Cirino, R. J., and Beck, S. J. "Social Information Processing and the Effects of Reputational, Situational, Developmental, and Gender Factors Among Children's Sociometric Groups." *Merrill-Palmer Quarterly,* 1991, *37,* 561–582.

Cohen, J. A. "A Coefficient of Agreement for Nominal Scales." *Educational and Psychological Measurement,* 1960, *20,* 37–46.

Coie, J. D. "Toward a Theory of Peer Rejection." In S. R. Asher and J. D. Coie (eds.), *Peer Rejection in Childhood* (pp. 365–401). New York: Cambridge University Press, 1990.

Coie, J. D., and Cillessen, A.H.N. "Peer Rejection: Origins and Effects on Children's Development." *Current Directions in Psychological Science,* 1993, *2,* 89–92.

Coie, J. D., and Dodge, K. A. "Continuities and Changes in Children's Social Status: A Five-Year Longitudinal Study." *Merrill-Palmer Quarterly,* 1983, *29,* 261–282.

Coie, J. D., Dodge, K. A., and Coppotelli, H. "Dimensions and Types of Social Status: A Cross-Age Perspective." *Developmental Psychology,* 1982, *18,* 557–570.

Coie, J. D., and Krehbiel, G. "Effects of Academic Tutoring on the Social Status of Low Achieving, Socially Rejected Children." *Child Development,* 1984, *55,* 1465–1478.

Coie, J. D., Lochman, J. E., Terry, R., and Hyman, C. "Predicting Early Adolescent Disorder from Childhood Aggression and Peer Rejection." *Journal of Consulting and Clinical Psychology*, 1992, 60, 783–792.

Coie, J. D., Terry, R., Lenox, K., Lochman, J. E., and Hyman, C. "Childhood Peer Rejection and Aggression as Predictors of Stable Patterns of Adolescent Disorder." *Development and Psychopathology*, 1995, 7, 697–713.

Crick, N. R., and Dodge, K. A. "A Review and Reformulation of Social Information-Processing Mechanisms in Children's Social Adjustment." *Psychological Bulletin*, 1994, 115, 74–101.

DeLawyer, D. D., and Foster, S. L. "The Effects of Peer Relationships on the Functions of Interpersonal Behavior in Children." *Journal of Clinical Child Psychology*, 1986, 15, 127–133.

DeRosier, M. E., Kupersmidt, J. B., and Patterson, C. J. "Children's Academic and Behavioral Adjustment as a Function of the Chronicity and Proximity of Peer Rejection." *Child Development*, 1994, 65, 1799–1813.

Dodge, K. A. "Social Cognition and Children's Aggressive Behavior." *Child Development*, 1980, 51, 162–170.

Dodge, K. A., and Frame, C. L. "Social Cognitive Biases and Deficits in Aggressive Boys." *Child Development*, 1982, 53, 620–635.

Franzoi, S. L., Davis, M. H., and Vasquez-Suson, K. A. "Two Social Worlds: Social Correlates and Stability of Adolescent Status Groups." *Journal of Personality and Social Psychology*, 1994, 67, 462–473.

Glidewell, J. C., Kantor, M. B., Smith, L. M., and Stringer, L. A. "Socialization and Social Structure in the Classroom." In M. L. Hoffman and L. W. Hoffman (eds.), *Review of Child Development Research* (pp. 221–256). New York: Russell Sage, 1966.

Gresham, F. M., and Nagle, R. J. "Social Skills Training with Children: Responsiveness to Modeling and Coaching as a Function of Peer Orientation." *Journal of Consulting and Clinical Psychology*, 1980, 48, 718–729.

Gresham, F. M., and Stuart, D. "Stability of Sociometric Assessment: Implications for Uses as Selection and Outcome Measures in Social Skills Training." *Journal of School Psychology*, 1992, 30, 223–231.

Gronlund, N. E. *Sociometry in the Classroom*. New York: Harper, 1959.

Harris, M. J., Milich, R., Johnston, E. M., and Hoover, D. W. "Effects of Expectancies on Children's Social Interactions." *Journal of Experimental Social Psychology*, 1990, 26, 1–12.

Hartup, W. W. "Peer Relations." In E. M. Hetherington (ed.) and P. H. Mussen (series ed.), *Handbook of Child Psychology: Vol. 4. Socialization, Personality, and Social Development* (pp. 103–196). New York: Wiley, 1983.

Hartup, W. W. "The Company They Keep: Friendships and Their Developmental Significance." *Child Development*, 1996, 67, 1–13.

Hubbard, J. A., and Coie, J. D. "Emotional Correlates of Social Competence in Children's Peer Relationships." *Merrill-Palmer Quarterly*, 1994, 40, 1–20.

Hymel, S. "Preschool Children's Peer Relations: Issues in Sociometric Assessment." *Merrill-Palmer Quarterly*, 1983, 29, 237–260.

Hymel, S. "Interpretations of Peer Behavior: Affective Bias in Childhood and Adolescence." *Child Development*, 1986, 57, 431–445.

La Greca, A. M., and Santogrossi, D. "Social Skills Training with Elementary School Students: A Behavioral Approach." *Journal of Consulting and Clinical Psychology*, 1980, 48, 220–227.

Ladd, G. W. "Effectiveness of a Social Learning Method For Enhancing Children's Social Interaction and Peer Acceptance." *Child Development*, 1981, 52, 171–178.

Landis, J. R., and Koch, G. G. "The Measurement of Observer Agreement for Categorical Data." *Biometrics*, 1977, 33, 159–174.

Lemann, T. B., and Solomon, R. L. "Group Characteristics as Revealed in Sociometric Patterns and Personality Ratings." *Sociometry*, 1952, 15, 7–90.

McConnell, S. R., and Odom, S. L. "Sociometrics: Peer-Referenced Measures and the Assessment of Social Competence." In P. S. Strain, M. J. Guralnick, and H. M. Walker (eds.), *Children's Social Behavior: Development, Assessment, and Modification* (pp. 216–284). New York: Academic Press, 1986.

Mize, J., and Ladd, G. W. "A Cognitive-Social Learning Approach to Social Skill Training with Low-Status Preschool Children." *Developmental Psychology*, 1990, *26*, 388–397.

Moreno, J. L. *Who Shall Survive? A New Approach to the Problem of Human Interrelations.* Washington, D.C.: Nervous and Mental Disease Publishing Co., 1934.

Musser, L. M., and Graziano, W. G. "Behavioral Confirmation in Children's Interactions with Peers." *Basic and Applied Social Psychology*, 1991, *12*, 441–456.

Newcomb, A. F., and Bukowski, W. M. "Social Impact and Social Preference as Determinants of Children's Peer Group Status." *Developmental Psychology*, 1983, *19*, 856–867.

Newcomb, A. F., and Bukowski, W. M. "A Longitudinal Study of the Utility of Social Preference and Social Impact Sociometric Classification Schemes." *Child Development*, 1984, *55*, 1434–1447.

Newcomb, A. F., Bukowski, W. M., and Pattee, L. "Children's Peer Relations: A Meta-Analytic Review of Popular, Rejected, Neglected, Controversial, and Average Sociometric Status." *Psychological Bulletin*, 1993, *113*, 99–128.

Northway, M. L. "Sociometry and Some Challenging Problems of Social Relationships." *Sociometry*, 1946, *9*, 187–198.

Oden, S., and Asher, S. R. "Coaching Children in Social Skills for Friendship Making." *Child Development*, 1977, *48*, 495–506.

Ollendick, T. H., Greene, R. W., Francis, G., and Baum, C. G. "Sociometric Status: Its Stability and Validity Among Neglected, Rejected, and Popular Children." *Journal of Child Psychology and Psychiatry*, 1991, *32*, 525–534.

Olson, S. L. "Development of Conduct Problems and Peer Rejection in Preschool Children: A Social Systems Analysis." *Journal of Abnormal Child Psychology*, 1992, *20*, 327–350.

Parker, J. G., and Asher, S. R. "Peer Relations and Later Personal Adjustment: Are Low-Accepted Children at Risk?" *Psychological Bulletin*, 1987, *102*, 357–389.

Peery, J. "Popular, Amiable, Isolated, Rejected: A Reconceptualization of Sociometric Status in Preschool Children." *Child Development*, 1979, *50*, 1231–1234.

Pepinsky, P. N. "The Meaning of 'Validity' and 'Reliability' as Applied to Sociometric Tests." *Educational and Psychological Measurement*, 1949, *9*, 39–49.

Pettit, G., Clawson, M. A., Dodge, K. A., and Bates, J. E. "Stability and Change in Peer-Rejected Status: The Role of Child Behavior, Parenting, and Family Ecology." *Merrill-Palmer Quarterly*, 1996, *42*, 267–294.

Rabiner, D., and Coie, J. D. "Effect of Expectancy Inductions on Rejected Children's Acceptance by Unfamiliar Peers." *Developmental Psychology*, 1989, *25*, 450–457.

Renshaw, P. D., and Brown, P. J. "Loneliness in Middle Childhood: Concurrent and Longitudinal Predictors." *Child Development*, 1993, *64*, 1271–1284.

Rogosch, F. A., and Newcomb, A. F. "Children's Perceptions of Peer Reputations and Their Social Reputations Among Peers." *Child Development*, 1989, *60*, 597–610.

Rosenthal, R. "Interpersonal Expectancy Effects: A 30-Year Perspective." *Current Directions in Psychological Science*, 1994, *3*, 176–179.

Snyder, M. "When Beliefs Create Reality." In L. Berkowitz (ed.), *Advances in Experimental Social Psychology* (Vol. 18, pp. 248–306). New York: Academic Press, 1984.

Swann, W. B., Jr. "Self-Verification: Bringing Social Reality into Harmony with the Self." In J. Suls and A. G. Greenwald (eds.), *Psychological Perspectives on the Self* (Vol. 2, pp. 33–66). Hillsdale, N.J.: Erlbaum, 1983.

Swann, W. B., Jr. "Identity Negotiation: Where Two Roads Meet." *Journal of Personality and Social Psychology*, 1987, *53*, 1038–1051.

Terry, R., and Coie, J. D. "A Comparison of Methods for Defining Sociometric Status Among Children." *Developmental Psychology*, 1991, *27*, 867–880.

Vaughn, B. E., and Mize, J. "A Comparison of Two Methods for Estimating Sociometric Status in Preschool-Age Children." Paper presented at the biennial meeting of the Society for Research in Child Development, Seattle, Apr. 1991.

Vitaro, F., Gagnon, C., and Tremblay, R. E. "Predicting Stable Peer Rejection from Kindergarten to Grade One." *Journal of Clinical Child Psychology*, 1990, *19*, 257–264.

Vitaro, F., Tremblay, R. E., Gagnon, C., and Boivin, M. "Peer Rejection from Kindergarten to Grade 2: Outcomes, Correlates, and Prediction." *Merrill-Palmer Quarterly*, 1992, *38*, 382–400.

Williams, B.T.R., and Gilmour, J. D. "Annotation: Sociometry and Peer Relationships." *Journal of Child Psychology and Psychiatry*, 1994, *35*, 997–1013.

Witryol, S. L., and Thompson, G. G. "A Critical Review of the Stability of Social Acceptability Scores Obtained with the Partial-Rank-Order and the Paired-Comparison Scales." *Genetic Psychology Monographs*, 1953, *48*, 221–260.

Wright, J. C., Giammarino, M., and Parad, H. W. "Social Status in Small Groups: Individual-Group Similarity and the Social 'Misfit.'" *Journal of Personality and Social Psychology*, 1986, *50*, 523–536.

ANTONIUS H. N. CILLESSEN is associate professor in the Department of Psychology of the University of Connecticut.

WILLIAM M. BUKOWSKI is professor in the Department of Psychology of Concordia University, Montreal.

GERBERT J. T. HASELAGER is a postdoctoral fellow in the Rutten Institute for Research in Psychology at the University of Nijmegen, The Netherlands.

INDEX

Northway, M. L., 5, 9, 37, 38, 49–50, 52, 76, 92
Notice score, 7
Novick, M. R., 36, 37, 52

Oden, S., 30, 52, 88, 92
Odom, S. L., 76, 92
Ollendick, T. H., 78–79, 80, 92
Olson, S. L., 78–79, 85, 92
Optimal scaling, 37

Paired comparisons, 31, 32–33
Parad, H. W., 30, 48, 52, 53, 84, 93
Parker, J. G., 21, 26, 48, 50, 53, 84, 86, 92
Pattee, L., 56, 72, 84, 92
Patterson, C. J., 86, 91
PC-BILOG program, 40–41, 42
PC-MULTILOG program, 40–41
Peer groups, dynamic nature of, 5
Peer-nomination method, 31
Peer rating method, 31, 32
Peery, J., 7, 10, 55, 60, 72, 76, 92
Pepinsky, P. N., 36–37, 53, 89, 92
Pettit, G., 78–79, 86, 92
Pizzmiglio, M. T., 25
Popular children, 7–8
Poteat, M. G., 76, 90
Powell, M., 7, 8, 10
Preference, as derivative sociometric construct, 13–14
Price, J. M., 35, 48, 50, 53
Probabilistic considerations, versus conceptual concerns, 8–9
Psychometric validity research, 35–37
Pyszczynski, T., 37, 53

Rabiner, D., 85, 92
Rank-order method, 31–32
Rasch, G., 40, 43, 45, 53
Rating scales, 15–17
Ratings: in longitudinal research, 66–69; nomination procedures versus, 60–66; and two-dimensional sociometric status determination, 55–71; usefulness of, 57–60
Rejected children, 8, 9
Rejection: differential variability in, 14–18; interrelationship of acceptance and, 14–18; linear and curvilinear association between acceptance and, 18–20. See also Repulsion

Renshaw, P. D., 84, 92
Repulsion: Moreno definition of, 3–4; in studies of the 1940s and 1950s, 5–7
Rogosch, F. A., 85, 92
Rosenthal, R., 21, 22, 26, 85, 92
Rubin, D. B., 21, 22, 26, 48, 50, 53

Santogrossi, D., 88, 91
Scale scores, deriving, 46–47
Scott, J., 33, 53
Singleton, L. C., 32, 53
Sippola, L., 1, 11
Smith, L. M., 75, 91
Snyder, M., 85, 92
Social expansivity construct, 31
Social impact dimension, 7. See also Impact
Social isolation construct, 31
Social network analysis, 33
Social preference dimension, 7
Social sensitivity, 44–46
Social visibility, 34
Sociometric categories: children's age and interval length in, 82–83; explanation for stability of, 84–86; and long-term stability, 81–82; responsiveness of, to change, 88; and short-term stability, 81; stability of, 76–83; and stability of two-dimensional classification systems, 77–81; and two-dimensional classification systems, 76–77
Sociometric constructs, derivative, 13–14
Sociometric judgment: application of, to child psychology, 5–8; basic ideas underlying Moreno's model of, 3–5; bilateralness of Moreno's model for, 9; Bronfenbrenner's technique for, 5–6; classification systems for, 7; Lemann and Solomon's taxonomy for, 6–7; limitations of current systems of, 8–9
Sociometric measures: historical issues and, 28–29; and interrelationship between acceptance and rejection, 12–14; and issue of nomination and rating scale measures indexing the same construct, 14–18; issues regarding use of, 11–25; stimulus-aspect differences in, 29–30
Sociometric status determination, two-dimensional, 55–71

Back Issue/Subscription Order Form

Copy or detach and send to:
Jossey-Bass, 350 Sansome Street, San Francisco, CA 94104-1342

Call or fax toll free!
Phone 888-378-2537 6AM–5PM PST; Fax 800-605-2665

Back issues: Please send me the following issues at $25 each
(Important: please include series initials and issue number, such as CD88)

1. CD _____

_____

_____

$ _____ Total for single issues

$$ _____ Shipping charges (for single issues *only;* subscriptions are exempt
from shipping charges): Up to $30, add $5.50 • $30.01–$50, add $6.50
$50.01–$75, add $8 • $75.01–$100, add $10 • $100.01–$150, add $12
Over $150, call for shipping charge

Subscriptions   Please ❑ start   ❑ renew my subscription to *New Directions
for Child and Adolescent Development* for the year _____ at the
following rate:

U.S.:   ❑ Individual $67   ❑ Institutional $115

Canada: ❑ Individual $92   ❑ Institutional $140

All others: ❑ Individual $97   ❑ Institutional $145

NOTE: Subscriptions are quarterly, and are for the calendar year only.
Subscriptions begin with the Spring issue of the year indicated above.

$ _____ Total single issues and subscriptions (Add appropriate sales tax for
your state for single issues. No sales tax on U.S. subscriptions.
Canadian residents add GST for subscriptions and single issues.)

❑ Payment enclosed (U.S. check or money order only)

❑ VISA, MC, AmEx, Discover Card #_____ Exp. date_____

Signature _____ Day phone _____

❑ Bill me (U.S. institutional orders only. Purchase order required)

Purchase order #_____

Federal Tax ID 135593032 GST 89102-8502

Name _____

Address _____

_____

Phone_____ E-mail _____

For more information about Jossey-Bass, visit our Web site at:
www.josseybass.com   **PRIORITY CODE = ND1**